詩林明理
古今抒情詩160首

Parallel Reading of 160 Classical
and New Chinese Lyrical Poemxus
漢英對照
Chinese-English

張智中譯　Translator: Zhang Zhizhong
林明理著　Author:　　　Lin Mingli

文史哲英譯叢刊
文史哲出版社印行

國家圖書館出版品預行編目資料

詩林明理：古今抒情詩 160 首 / 林明理著；
　張智中譯 -- 初版 -- 臺北市：文史哲，
　民 112.03
　　頁；公分（文史哲英譯叢刊；7）
中英對照
ISBN 978-986-314-637-7（平裝）

831.　　　　　　　　　　112005214

文史哲英譯叢刊　　　7

詩林明理：古今抒情詩 160 首

著　　者：林　　　明　　　理
譯　　者：張　　　智　　　中
出 版 者：文　史　哲　出　版　社
　　　　　http://www.lapen.com.tw
　　　　　e-mail：lapen@ms74.hinet.net
登記證字號：行政院新聞局版臺業字五三三七號
發 行 人：彭　　　　正　　　　雄
發 行 所：文　史　哲　出　版　社
印 刷 者：文　史　哲　出　版　社
臺北市羅斯福路一段七十二巷四號
郵政劃撥帳號：一六一八○一七五
電話 886-2-23511028・傳真 886-2-23965656

實價新臺幣五二○元

二 ○ 二 三 年（民 112）四 月 初 版

詩 林 明 理

古今抒情詩160首

目　次

詩 林 明 理

古今抒情詩 *160* 首

Parallel Reading of 160 Classical and New Chinese Lyrical Poems

漢英對照 Chinese-English

英譯：張智中　　Translator:　Zhang Zhizhong
新詩：林明理　　Author:　　　Lin Mingli

Poetry is a lifelong war waged
against ineffable beauty.
by Atticus

詩歌乃是一場終生的戰爭
向著難以言說之美
阿提卡斯

前　言

　　為了打開讀者進入古詩及新詩學習的門徑，本書由現任南開大學外國語學院博士生導師張智中教授悉心精選中國古詩八十首，並由臺灣學者林明理博士以新詩延伸的方式，嘗試讓海內外熱愛詩歌的讀者，能欣賞到中英對照的詩美意境。我們期盼本書能夠讓閱讀詩歌成為通向每一個讀者心靈愉悅的道路。

張智中、林明理 謹識
2023 年 1 月 26 日

Foreword

In order to open the door for readers to learn classical and new Chinese poems, professor Zhang Zhizhong, doctoral supervisor in the College of Foreign Languages of Nankai University, has selected 80 classical Chinese poems, each coupled with a new poem written by Dr. Lin Mingli, a famous poet and scholar from Taiwan. This kind of classical Chinese poems coupled with new Chinese poems as an extension in reading, plus English translations, is somewhat original. The book aims to solicit the readers' interest and passion in appreciating the beautiful artistic conception of Chinese-English poetry. It is hoped that this book, beginning in classical and new Chinese poems as well as their English translations, can end in delighting the soul of the readers.

By **Zhang Zhizhong** & **Lin Mingli**
January, 26, 2023

導 言

　　林明理老師是臺灣著名詩人和學者，根據自己的所感所悟，及其古詩閱讀的經驗回憶，她根據精選的 80 首古詩，從自己的新詩創作中進行篩選、配對，並附在編譯的古詩之後，以期望讀者更貼近地感受和瞭解詩美的世界。我們認為，若能讓古詩和新詩研究同步進行，相輔相成，讓翻譯詩歌的涵義變得更加生動活潑，可使學生在欣賞詩歌與研讀上產生莫大的興趣，這是此書最重要的閱讀價值，也可加深閱讀過程中的感性和體悟，這也是我們的期許。新詩的英譯，雖有變通，一般做到行行對應；古詩的英譯，卻因詩制宜，採取不同的外在形式，並時有深層之譯。譯詩之趣，讀者自可體會玩味。

張智中
2023 年 1 月 23 日於
天津明月松間居

Introduction

Dr. Lin Mingli is a famous poet and scholar from Taiwan, and she conscientiously selects 80 poems written by her, to match the 80 classical Chinese poems according to her experience of life and feeling in poetry reading, in order for the readers to more intimately enjoy the world of poetic aesthetics. It is our belief that the simultaneous study of classical and new Chinese poems is supplementary or reciprocal, and it can lend more charm to the corresponding English translations, and more interest to the students during their course of appreciating and studying poetry. This is the most important value of the book, where the readers can be enlightened concerning their poetry sensibility and understanding, and this is also our expectation. As for the translation of new poems by Lin Mingli, a line-to-line correspondence is generally observed in spite of occasional adaptations and changes; in the English translation of classical Chinese poems, different poetic forms are taken to better bring out the poetic beauty in the original pieces, and deep translation is applied sometimes to guarantee a good poem. The readers, reading this book from cover to cover, can easily feel the pleasure and charm of poetry translation.

Zhang Zhizhong
Residence of Moon-Peering Pines, Tianjin
January 23, 2023

1. 登樂游原

唐·李商隱

向晚意不適，
驅車登古原。
夕陽無限好，
只是近黃昏。

1. Ascending the Pleasure Plateau

Li Shangyin [Tang Dynasty]

Late in the afternoon, as the dim ball
of the sun is sinking slowly in the horizon,
I feel out of sorts and drive a chariot
to the ancient plateau where the sunny
beauty knows no bounds before it fades
to be fainter, paler, and dimmer ....

Translator: Zhang Zhizhong

在匆匆一瞥間

林明理

黃昏的海鳥拍動著寒意…
我們的腳步聲
恍若越過潮汐和許多山峰，
從紅牆的迴廊樹蔭，
到落日睞著銀藍的眼瞳。

我好想停在山的高處，
像馬兒豎起耳朵—
聽聽朝向彼端海岸的天空，
然後一派輕鬆地…
…親近了你，這就是我。

A Fleeting Glimpse

Lin Mingli

The seabirds at dusk are fluttering with a chill ...
The sound of our footfalls
Seemingly rises over the tides and a host of peaks,
From the tree shadows in the red-walled cloister,
To the setting sun that is squinting its silver-blue eye.

How I want to stay on the height of the mountain,
Like a horse pricking up its ears —
Listen to the sky stretching toward the coast beyond,
Then with great ease ....
... Walk close to you, and this is me.

Translator: Zhang Zhizhong

2. 訪人不遇留別館

唐·李商隱

卿卿不惜鎖窗春，
去作長楸走馬身。
閑倚繡簾吹柳絮，
日高深院斷無人。

2. Staying at an Inn After Failure to Be Taken in by a Friend

Li Shangyin [Tang Dynasty]

Oh my loving friend, oh
my beloved pal, why, instead
    of cherishing a gardenful of
splendid spring, should you,
riding a horse, trudge and traipse
    along a long way lined with
        lingering catalpa trees?

In helpless idleness, I lean
against the balustrade fanned
    by the wind-blown embroidered
curtain of the inn, where fluffy
catkin pieces are dancing
    in the languid air, to fix my gaze
on the yonder deep yard, which,
deserted by you, is bathed in
    lonely sunlight and vacant spring.

Translator: Zhang Zhizhong

在驀然回首時

林明理

當愛情站在我面前，
我選擇相信奇蹟──
奮勇向前
或努力就能成就好事；

春天來了，
風如此甜美，雨如此親切；
我愛它突如其來的朝氣，
也試著理解它是多麼地難以捉摸；

而今，世間一片寧靜，
回過頭來，
那越顯清晰的身影──是誰呢？
啊，原來是風，──

它對著我的耳朵，
吹著一抹淺笑，
在此刻，月兒從樹梢移過：
溫馨而靜好。

When Suddenly I Look Back

Lin Mingl

When love stands before me,
I choose to believe in miracles —
Go ahead with courage
Or with efforts, and achievements can be accomplished;

Spring is around the corner,
The wind is so sweet, and the rain so gentle;
I love its sudden vitality,
And try to understand its elusiveness;

Today, the world is quietude itself,
When I look back,
A form is more and more distinct — who could it be?
Oh, it turns out to be the wind.

Into or against my ears,
It is blowing with a gentle smile,
Now, the moon is moving over the treetops:
Warm, and nice.

Translator: Zhang Zhizhong

3. 無　題

唐・李商隱

相見時難別亦難，
東風無力百花殘。
春蠶到死絲方盡，
蠟炬成灰淚始幹。
曉鏡但愁雲鬢改，
夜吟應覺月光寒。
蓬山此去無多路，
青鳥殷勤為探看。

3. Untitled

Li Shangyin [Tang Dynasty]

It is hard for us to meet
and difficult to bid adieu;
languid east wind blows
a hundred withered flowers.
Spring silkworm vomits silk
until it dies; the candle
refuses to dry its tears
until burnt into ashes.
The morning mirror
worries about graying hair;
night chanting must feel
the chill of moonlight.
The road to immortal
Mount Penglai is cut off;
Blue Bird, please visit her
and send my regards.

Translator: Zhang Zhizhong

如風往事

林明理

終究
一切都已結束
終究
讓愛遠飆
終究
獨自步上荊棘之路
我的靈魂懸在崖壁
　　邊游邊躲

是誰
讓一切返回虛無
是誰
兀自矗立懸崖之後
不再夢寐以求什麼
愛，可以反覆難測
也可以歸於平淡
　　來去無蹤

Gone with the Wind

Lin Mingli

Eventually
Everything is over
Eventually
For love to float away
Eventually
Alone on the thorny road
My soul is hanging over the cliff
    Wandering and evading

Who is it
For everything to return to nothingness
Who is it
Standing alone behind the cliff
No longer dreaming of anything
Love, can be fathomed time and again
And it can be ignored in spite of
    Its willful coming and going

Translator: Zhang Zhizhong

4. 題都城南莊

唐・崔護

去年今日此門中，
人面桃花相映紅。
人面不知何處去，
桃花依舊笑春風。

4 . Written on the Wall of the Village

Cui Hu [Tang Dynasty]

This day, last year, before
this very door, peach blossoms
  blush in the gentle breeze,
against the blush of a pretty
girl. But now where is her
  fair face? — only peach

petals are beaming
and smiling in
  the spring breeze.

Translator: Zhang Zhizhong

在每個山水之間

林明理

這一片憂鬱的草原啊永遠延續著
古老的疏林
當月亮模糊而遙遠之影
躲進了峻嶺，卻有個聲音
在每個山水之間飄蕩不停
那是鋪滿了泥草的神秘老城
在淒然的冬日
以蹲踞姿勢窺視
所有生物的流動之聲

我向所有的星宿裡探尋
它們深切目光使我心兒悲痛
每當冰和雪裹上了壘石的長徑
草原的歌聲便以它的柔波
使我在睡夢中恍惚清醒
啊那大地之詩啊已掠過微芒的東方
讓我不再佇足嘆息

愛情的幻變哀音

Among Hills and Rills

Lin Mingli

Oh the melancholy grassland stretches forever
The ancient sparse woods
When the dim and distant form of the moon
Hides itself in lofty peaks, there is a voice
Which is on the wafting among hills and rills
It is the mysterious ancient city choked with mud and
grass
In miserable wintry days
Peeking while squatting
The running voices of all life-forms

I pry into all the stars
Their solicitous eyes bring sorrow into my heart
Whenever ice and snow blanket the long path of
stones
With their soft waves the grassland songs bring
A trance and a sense of wakefulness in my dream
Oh the poetry of earth has flashed in the east
beginning to be bright with light
For me not to stop for sighs
The changeable lamentations of love

Translator: Zhang Zhizhong

5. 憶江南

唐・白居易

江南好，
風景舊曾諳。
日出江花紅勝火，
春來江水綠如藍，
能不憶江南？

5. Remembering the Southern Shore

Bai Juyi [Tang Dynasty]

Fair is the Southern Shore,

with whose view I have been familiar:

at sunrise river-side flowers blossom like fire;

in spring the river water is a profound blue.

How can I refrain from remembering the Southern Shore?

Translator: Zhang Zhizhong

冥　想

林明理

多思慕你

邊馳騁，邊微笑

像飛魚在水花間躍動

這是因為有普羅旺斯

夏日才這般夢幻

還是山丘上那片愛情花海

讓我斜倚著，向宇宙說話

Meditation

Lin Mingli

How I envy you

Galloping and smiling

Like flying fish flashing in the splashing water

It is because of Provence

Summer is so dreamy

Still the field of flowers of love on the hill

Against which I lean, while talking to the universe

Translator: Zhang Zhizhong

6. 相見歡‧烏夜啼

唐‧李煜

無言獨上西樓，
月如鉤。
寂寞梧桐深院鎖清秋。

剪不斷，理還亂，
是離愁。
別是一般滋味在心頭。

6. Joy at Meeting

Li Yu [Tang Dynasty]

Wordless, I mount the West Tower:
a hook is the moon.
Lonely parasol trees in the deep courtyard,
where a clear autumn has been locked.

Cutting, it is still connecting;
combing, it is still entangling.
This parting grief, how to purge?
The attempts have been ineffectual:
it weighs heavily on my mind,
unnameable, unutterable,
and untellable.

Translator: Zhang Zhizhong

秋雨，總是靜靜地下著⋯⋯

林明理

十月最後的一抹暮色
一切都是那麼寧靜
一隻黑鳥悄悄靠近
又悄悄離開
哦　朋友
⋯⋯我沒有忘記
又怎能忘記⋯⋯
我似鼓翼的蛾
努力向前
永不墜落
也許，你也在夜雨中
等待雲霧散開
讓我想像
在遙遠的過去
我們曾經一起
走入光芒裡
你的輕言細語
讓我滿耳充滿幸福

Quietly Falls the Autumn Rain ...

Lin Mingli

The last twilight of October
All is tranquility itself
A black bird stealthily approaches
Before leaving quietly
Oh my friend
... I have not forgotten
How can it be forgettable ...
Like a fluttering moth
I strive to move on
Never to drop down
Maybe you are also in the night rain
Waiting for the fog and clouds to clear up
For me to imagine
In the remote past
We have ever walked together
Into the rays of light
Your gentle whispers
Fill my ears with happiness

Translator: Zhang Zhizhong

7. 劍門道中遇微雨

宋・陸遊

衣上征塵雜酒痕，
遠遊無處不消魂。
此身合是詩人未？
細雨騎驢入劍門。

7. Caught in a Drizzle on the Way

Lu You [Tang Dynasty]

Weary and travel-worn from
a good bit of a journey made
　　　today, I am in a bad state of
my clothes, which are soiled
with dust and stains of wine;
　　　yet travelling faraway, to any
place, is ravishing. Self-reflection:
am I equal to the name of a poet?
　　　Riding a donkey, I, drenched
in the drizzling rain, enter
the Sword Gate Pass, the
　　　greatest pass in the world.

Translator: Zhang Zhizhong

路

林明理

一條無盡的路
橫臥在巨峰之間。
僅少數的村人，僧侶
沿著這路蜿蜒向前……

擁抱世界的夢想，
從青春的少年
到孤獨的暮年，
生命轉瞬即逝；

蒼天許我以歌——
像隻黑頭文鳥
在田野中自由飛翔，
領受大地賜給我的恩典。

The Road

Lin Mingli

An endless road
Lies between mountain peaks.
Only a few villagers and monks
Are walking along the meandering road ...

The dream of embracing the world,
From the children of youth
To the lonely old age,
Life is fleeting and momentary;

Heaven gives me songs —
Like a blackbird
Flying freely in the fields,
Receiving the favors bestowed upon me from the earth

Translator: Zhang Zhizhong

8. 生查子‧元夕

宋‧歐陽修

去年元夜時，
花市燈如畫。
月上柳梢頭，
人約黃昏後。

今年元夜時，
月與燈依舊。
不見去年人，
淚濕春衫袖。

8. Lantern Festival Again

Ouyang Xiu [Song Dynasty]

Last year, last lantern festival,
the flowery fair is brilliantly lit like a broad
day: my sweetie and I meet after the afternoon,
when the moon is effectual through the willows ....

This year, this evening, as it darkens a variety of gay-colored
lamps are lit as brilliantly as the moon, casting rays of light,
which fails to fall full upon her fair face —
I am beside myself with sentimentality,
and my spring sleeves are soaked
with tears dripping
and dropping

Translator: Zhang Zhizhong

我將獨行

林明理

多少次
我們走過這小徑，
月寂寂。山脈諦聽著海音
夜鷺緩踱

大海看似平靜
肥沃的田野睡在星輝中
總是相視、無語
細碎的足聲踏響整個天際

今日，我將獨行——
依然走在這條舊路
你已遠去，而我心悠悠
重逢是未來歲月的憂愁

I Will Walk Alone

Lin Mingli

How many times
We have walked along the path,
The moon silent. Mountains are listening to the sound
of the sea,
When a night heron is pacing slowly

The sea seems calm
The fertile field is sleeping in the starlight
Looking at each other, always wordless
The gentle footfalls are echoing beyond the sky

Today, I will walk alone —
Still along the old path
You are far away, my heart pining;
Reunion is the worries of future years.

Translator: Zhang Zhizhong

9. 塞下曲（其三）

唐·盧綸

月黑雁飛高，
單于夜遁逃。
欲將輕騎逐，
大雪滿弓刀。

凝望

林明理

穿越巨浪
時間的海鷗
正叼走一頁滄史

9. *Border Songs* *(No. 3)*

Lu Lun [Tang Dynasty]

In moonless night the wild geese
fly high, when invaders flee away
in a flurry under the cover of night,
to be lost in darkness and distance.
Cavalrymen are on the point of pursuing
when, on the instant, come the sweep
and flash of their bows & swords,
which are burdened with heavy snow.

Gazing

Lin Mingli

Through huge waves
The seagulls of time
Are carrying away in their beaks a page of surging history

Translator: Zhang Zhizhong

10. 鹿 柴

唐·王維

空山不見人，
但聞人語響。
返景入深林，
複照青苔上。

10. A Secluded Forest Scene

Wang Wei [Tang Dynasty]

Not a single soul is seen
in the empty mountain —
save some whispering,
the echoing sound as of
a human voice — where
a wandering shaft of light,
through lacing boughs of
the forest, is flickering and
trickling down, broken and
subdued to soft light,
before falling full upon
the green moss aground.

Translator: Zhang Zhizhong

寂靜的遠山

林明理

寂靜的遠山
夜鶯，枝椏，落葉掃著水面
我以詩
漫射出甜美的語言
歌唱比微笑更顯著的夜空
那細微的鈴聲，隱隱傳來
——是牧羊人回家了

Silent Remote Mountains

Lin Mingli

Silent remote mountains

Nightingales, branches, leaves are skimming the water

In a poem

I emanate sweet words

To sing the night sky which is more prominent than a smile

The subtle tinkling of bells travels here faintly

—— The shepherd is going home

Translator: Zhang Zhizhong

11. 如夢令

宋・李清照

昨夜雨疏風驟，

濃睡不消殘酒。

試問捲簾人，

卻道海棠依舊。

知否，

知否？

應是綠肥紅瘦。

愛

林明理

我不能說，我不懂愛情的

幻變與詩意

但你絕對像星辰般——

閃耀，卻那麼飄渺難尋

11. A Dreamy Song

Li Qingzhao [Song Dynasty]

Last night sees sporadic rain and gusts of wind;
deep sleep fails to rid me of the wine's effect.
I ask the screen roller about the yardful of cherry-apple
blossoms,
and the reply: they are still nice and fair, but
you shall know,
you shall know:
against red, green is now prevailing.

Love

Lin Mingli

I can't say that I don't understand love

Fantasy and poetry

But you are absolutely like a star —

Twinkling, yet so ethereally hard to trace

要我調侃地說：
其實愛情需要一點隱密
它總是不經意地出現……
……意在言外的妙趣

我也想像隻琴鳥
以自然的方式——
照看森林，自由呼吸
或渴望諦聽大地的低語

偶爾想遠遠飛到樹梢
或躲在閣樓裡——
恣意地想像或專注地
翻閱一本詩集

我不能說，我不懂愛情的
燦爛與憂鬱
它像史詩般魔幻，想著
想著——就莫名歡喜

Let me say jokingly:
Actually love needs a little secret
It comes all unawares …
…The fun lies beyond the words

I also want to be like a lyrebird
In a natural way —
To see to the forest and breathe freely
Or eager to listen to the whispers of the earth

Occasionally I want to fly to the treetop
Or to hide in an attic —
To abandon myself to imagination or attentively
Read a poetry book

I can't say that I don't understand love
Brilliant or melancholy
It is magic like an epic, thinking
Thinking and thinking — and joyful inexplicably

Translator: Zhang Zhizhong

12. 竹裡館

唐・王維

獨坐幽篁裡，
彈琴複長嘯。
深林人不知，
明月來相照。

12. A Retreat in Bamboos

Wang Wei [Tang Dynasty]

Alone I sit in a secluded
grove of shady bamboos:
I play my lute while whistling
along. In the depths of woods
no one knows I am here,
and I am privy to none
but the bright moon, who
is my boon companion.

Translator: Zhang Zhizhong

冬之歌*

林明理

月光漫過草的山巔

積雪覆蓋石頭和溪流

此刻，星空覆蓋的多洛米蒂

散發純淨的光

讓我內心無比地平和

*義大利北邊多洛米蒂（The
Dolomites）在 2009 年被列入世
界自然遺產。

Winter Song

Lin Mingli

Moonlight flows over the grassy mountaintop

Snow covers up the stones and streams

Now, the sky over the Dolomites

Is shedding a pure light

Which lends great peace to my inner heart

Note: Dolomites, a mountain range in north Italy, was listed as one of the World Natural Heritage Sites in 2009.

Translator: Zhang Zhizhong

13. 聲聲慢

宋·李清照

尋尋覓覓，
冷冷清清，
淒淒慘慘戚戚。
乍暖還寒時候，
最難將息。
三杯兩盞淡酒，
怎敵他晚來風急！
雁過也，
正傷心，
卻是舊時相識。

滿地黃花堆積，
憔悴損，
如今有誰堪摘？
守著窗兒，
獨自怎生得黑！
梧桐更兼細雨，
到黃昏，
點點滴滴。
這次第，
怎一個愁字了得！

13. A Slow Song after Another Slow Song

Li Qingzhao [Song Dynasty]

Searching after vain searching,
out of sorts, in a bad mood,
a feeling of frustration from frustration.
Now warm and then cold —
most difficult to fare well.
One or two or three cups of wine:
how to bear the brunt of an evening gale?
It is heartbreaking to see
a bevy of wild geese in flight,
which are my old acquaintances.

The ground is golden with a carpet of flowers:
a faded mass after another mass —
now, where are the pickers?
Looking through the lonely window —
hard to endure the tough time till dark!
The parasol trees are shivering in a drizzling rain,
the hours dragging along tediously
till dusk, dripping, and dropping ….
Such it is, how —
to bundle it off with a single word "sorrow"?

Translator: Zhang Zhizhong

致愛情

林明理

原來愛
無法裝傻或受阻攔
有時，心會不覺地
徜徉於樂曲中
或如疫後重生
不可言喻地歡喜

凡人只聽到
那愛神之箭斷折
卻看不清
愛情的未解之謎
還日夜認真等待
而我漸漸明白

愛
根本無法理解
更沒有重來
當愛情變成桑田滄海
它的回聲
響在空曠的天空上

To Love

Lin Mingli

Actually, in love
Lovers cannot play the fool or be stopped
Sometimes, unknowingly the heart
Is wandering in music
Or to be reborn from an epidemic
Joyful beyond words

Mortals can only hear
The snapping sound of the arrow of love
But they fail to see
The unsolved mystery of love
And they are patiently waiting day and night
When I gradually come to see it

Love
Defies any understanding
And it can never be relived
When love brings great changes to the world
Its echo
Is ringing in the boundlessly blue sky

Translator: Zhang Zhizhong

14. 相 思

唐・王維

紅豆生南國，
春來發幾枝？`
願君多採擷，
此物最相思。

14. Missing Afar

Wang Wei [Tang Dynasty]

Red beans grow in southern land;
how many twigs sprout in spring?
I wish you gather them as many as you
can, which are the token of true love.

Translator: Zhang Zhizhong

思念似雪花緘默地飛翔

林明理

思念似雪花緘默地飛翔
從地球彼端
沿著一條直線
穿越長長的山巒和河水
來回走動
引我期盼
就這樣把它迎進了門窗

我是顆渺小的水滴
自我耽溺於
一片廣闊的天空
當我緩緩地搖晃
落在大雪漫天的夜晚
啊，我想要歡呼
有什麼比得上你強大的靈魂
和那神采奕奕的光芒

Thoughts Fly Silently Like Snowflakes

Lin Mingli

Thoughts fly silently like snowflakes
From the other side of the earth
Along a straight line
Through long and meandering rivers and mountains
Back and forth
Soliciting my expectation
To welcome them into my door and window

I am a tiny drop of water
Self-indulged
In a boundless sky
When I slowly shake and shiver
Into the night veiled with heavy snow
Ah, I want to cheer and acclaim
What is comparable to your powerful soul
And your radiant light

Translator: Zhang Zhizhong

15. 山 行

唐・杜牧

遠上寒山石徑斜，
白雲深處有人家。
停車坐愛楓林晚，
霜葉紅於二月花。

15. A Mountain Trip

Du Mu [Tang Dynasty]

A winding path leads upward,
heavenward, for a considerable
  portion of which there are
  no houses lying near the road
except straggling stones, until
  I clamber to the cold mountaintop, to find a lofty residence
in the clouds of clouds. I stop
  my coach to admire eventide
  maple woods: frost-bitten
leaves are redder, redder than
  flowers of the third moon.

Translator: Zhang Zhizhong

黃 昏

林明理

越過綠野和海洋
我找到夕陽最後深情地一閃
正如四月桐鑲著雲彩
隱蔽於坡谷之下

Dusk

Lin Mingli

Over green fields and the ocean
I find the setting sun's final flash of profound affection
Just like the parasol trees in April, which are tinctured with clouds
Hidden in the deep valley

Translator: Zhang Zhizhong

16. 離思五首（之四）

唐・元稹

曾經滄海難為水，

除卻巫山不是雲。

取次花叢懶回顧，

半緣修道半緣君。

16. *Five Poems on My Strong Feeling of Affection* (No. 4)

Yuan Zhen [Tang Dynasty]

No water is water —

for a seafarer

who has seen the sea

overflowing with water;

no clouds are clouds

for a sightseer who

has seen Wushan Mountain

veiled in fluffy clouds.

Strolling through flowery

clusters, I do not deign

to dart a single loving look —

partly out of my religious cultivation,

partly out of my strong

feeling of affection for you.

Translator: Zhang Zhizhong

七月的思念

林明理

在山丘盡頭的
另一邊
無盡的海
岩岸的浪花
使我心悅

藍色的風
掠過
漁舟點點
聽鳥啁啾
我輕閉著眼

想念你
如候鳥翩躚
而你是
大河展延
我唯一的思念

Yearning in July

Lin Mingli

Beyond the end of
The hill
The boundless sea
The waves along the rocky shore
Greatly gladden me

The blue wind
Blows over
The fishing boats
I listen to the voice of the twittering birds
With eyes slightly closed

I miss you
Like the flying of a migrating bird
And you are
A long river which extends
My only longing and yearning

Translator: Zhang Zhizhong

17. 春 曉

唐・孟浩然

春眠不覺曉，
處處聞啼鳥。
夜來風雨聲，
花落知多少。

北京湖畔遐思

林明理

光的藏匿處
那片樹林前方的
薄冰層上

17. Glorious Spring Morning

Meng Haoran [Tang Dynasty]

A night, a rainy spring night,
is followed by a glorious
    morning, into which I am
    wakened, to inhale the fresh
morning air, to rejoice in the
    overflowing music of the birds
    and the fresh breath of the
early spring — a new creation
    from the nightlong winds and
rains. How many blossoms,
from the budding green of
    the woods, have been broken?

Reverie by the Lake of Beijing

Lin Mingli

The place where light hides
In front of the woods
On the thin ice

我所看到的是
陌生又熟悉——
美麗的雁鴨
翔集於此
在濕地的晨光中
似乎應和著什麼

沿著湖畔
風　盡情馳騁
在那兒前進著
而我卻感到如此溫暖
彷若　一顆心
徜徉在北國
與雪花一起掠過的
還有我所寄予
厚重的盼望

註：來自北京大學秦立彥教授捎來
信息及拍攝的野鴨照片，因而題詩
留念。

What I see is

The beautiful wild ducks —

Strange and familiar

They gather here

In the morning light of the wetland

Seemingly responding to something

Along the lakeshore

The wind　is coursing, galloping

And advancing

And I feel so warm

As if　a heart

Is wandering in the northland

Sweeping along with snowflakes

Are my eager

Expectations

Note: the poem is written upon receiving the message with photos of wild ducks from Professor Qin Liyan of Peking University.

Translator: Zhang Zhizhong

18. 逢雪宿芙蓉山主人

唐・劉長卿

日暮蒼山遠，
天寒白屋貧。
柴門聞犬吠，
風雪夜歸人。

18. A Night Arrival to the Cottage

Liu Changqing [Tang Dynasty]

Sundown, bleak hills remote; a white
cottage, wretched and forlorn, is sheltered
　under cold heavens. When I, with
　persistent determination, slowly and
steadily approach the door by dragging
　my weary body, I hear the barking, in
　soothing accents, of a dog, which abruptly
breaks the enveloping sheet of silence,
　while swelling melodiously in the fresh
air before dying away into the snowstorm
from which I am on the point of disengaging
　myself — to be a night arrival.

Translator: Zhang Zhizhong

二月春雪

林明理

這場雪景，
來自遙遠的芝加哥——
卻讓我感到無比的親切。
一排小樹，像一群
要去遠足的小孩，
屋內的詩人也不甘寂寞，
目不轉睛地打量著外面的世界。

夜晚
當大地睡着了。
雪啊，就繼續飛翔吧……
在後院裡飛翔，
飛入你深邃的眼睛，——
讓燈火點亮
你的詩意，
讓鳥獸們安息，
讓我整夜為你歌唱。

Spring Snow in February

Lin Mingli

This snowscape,
Is from the remote Chicago —
Yet it makes me feel so dear and familiar.
A row of small trees, like a group of
Children ready to for a hike;
The poet sitting in the room does not want to be left alone,
And he is looking intensely at the outside world.

At night,
The earth falls asleep
Oh, snow, continues to fly ...
Flying in the backyard,
Into your deep eyes, —
For the light to be on
To ignite your poetry,
For birds and beasts to sleep soundly,
For me to sing for you throughout the night.

Translator: Zhang Zhizhong

19. 長相思

清‧納蘭性德

山一程，
水一程，
身向榆關那畔行，
夜深千帳燈。

風一更，
雪一更，
聒碎鄉心夢不成，
故園無此聲。

19. Missing You Forever

Nalan Xingde[Qing Dynasty]

Over hills upon hills,

across rivers after rivers,

advancing and gaining upon Yu Guan Pass,

deep night sees thousands of tent camps brightened

by lamps.

Wind yelling and howling,

snow falling and swirling,

breaking and shattering my dream of sweet home,

to which such noises are strange.

Translator: Zhang Zhizhong

問 愛

林明理

在深不可測的眼神裡
我無法判斷
哪些是真實哪些是謊言

籃子裡的貓，瞇著眼
打了個呵欠
回答了所有的問題

牠懶洋洋地蹲伏於窗口
知道我無法逃遁

最後牠輕輕踱向我
彷彿愛情根本不存在過
除了這晦暗的雨中寧靜

About Love

Lin Mingli

In the unfathomable eyes
I cannot judge
What is truth and what is falsity

The cat in the basket, squinting its eyes
Makes a yawn
And have answered all the questions

It crouches lazily by the window
Knowing that I cannot escape

Finally it walks up to me
As if love never exists
Except tranquility in the gloomy rain

Translator: Zhang Zhizhong

20. 雪　梅

宋・盧梅坡

梅雪爭春未肯降，
騷人擱筆費評章。
梅須遜雪三分白，
雪卻輸梅一段香。

20. Mume Flowers & Snowy Blossoms

Lu Meipo [Song Dynasty]

The first sign of early spring:
mume flowers,
    or snowy blossoms?
Still an open question,
when the poet is
    a clumsy judge.
Mume flowers are inferior
to snowy blossoms in
    a stretch of white;
snowy blossoms are inferior
to mume flowers in
    a measure of fragrance.

Translator: Zhang Zhizhong

正月賞梅

林明理

　在都蘭山南麓鸞山村
沙沙枯葉聲和
　正月沃野的白梅香味
把所有煩囂都盡拋腦後
　雨後的五葉松更綠了
　雖然眾鳥寂靜
倘若你願意
　坐落在溪谷和部落之間
輕輕閉上眼
　而微風輕挑　梅雪皚皚
　大自然就是苦吟詩人

Admiring Plum Blossoms in January

Lin Mingli

In Nanshan Village to the south side of Dulan Mountain

The whistling sound of dried leaves

And the field fragrance of white plums in January

Leaves behind all the worries

The pines after a rainfall seem to be greener

Though the birds are silent

If you like

You can sit between the valley and the tribe

Gently close your eyes

When the gentle breeze is skittish over white snow on plum blossoms

The great nature is a bard with efforts

Translator: Zhang Zhizhong

21. 鵲橋仙

宋・秦觀

纖雲弄巧，

飛星傳恨，

銀漢迢迢暗度。

金風玉露一相逢，

便勝卻、人間無數。

柔情似水，

佳期如夢，

忍顧鵲橋歸路。

兩情若是久長時，

又豈在、朝朝暮暮。

21. Immortals at Magpie Bridge

Qin Guan [Song Dynasty]

The changing of flimsy clouds
is irregular and artful;
the shooting stars are pouring out
their missing and yearning.
Stealthily across the Silver River
the Cowherd meets the Weaving Girl.
A single annual meeting in the seventh
evening of the seventh month amidst
golden autumn wind & jade-glistening
dew puts to shame countless couples
in the mortal world.

Water-like tender feelings,
dreamy ecstatic tryst, at parting
how can they bear to look back
at the Magpie Bridge?
So long as two sweet hearts
are forever fondly in love,
why in the company of each other
from sweet morning to sweet
evening and from sweet evening
to sweet morning?

默 喚

林明理

在那鐘塔上
下望蜿蜒的河床，
小船兒點點
如碎銀一般！
彷彿從古老的風口裡
吹來一個浪漫的笛音，
穿越時空
驚起我心靈盤旋的
迴響。
我怎會忘記？
妳那凝思的臉，
伴隨這風中的淡香……
妳是我千年的期盼。
啊，布魯日，
小河裝著悠悠蕩漾的情傷，
而我，孤獨的，徘徊堤岸，
彷彿是中世紀才有著向晚！

Silent Calling

Lin Mingli

From the clock tower,
to overlook the meandering river,
which is dotted by small boats,
like scattered silver!
From the ancient wind
wafting here is a romantic fluting melody,
through time and space,
giving rise to a lingering echo
in my heart.

How can I forget
your pensive face
and the light fragrance in the wind?
You are my hope through thousands of years.
Oh, Bruges,
the small river is carrying the rippling sorrow,
when I, solitarily, wander along the bank,
as if in eventide only witnessed by the Middle Ages.

Translator: Zhang Zhizhong

22. 金鄉送韋八之西京

唐・李白

客自長安來，
還歸長安去。
狂風吹我心，
西掛咸陽樹。
此情不可道，
此別何時遇。
望望不見君，
連山起煙霧。

22. Bidding Farewell to My Friend

Li Bai [Tang Dynasty]

You are from the capital city
and now back to the capital city
you go; my heart is blown by
the wild wind, which bears my
heart away, westward, along
the route to be travelled by you,
among the trees which line the
road to escort you. My feelings,
stirred to their depths, are
unutterable, unspeakable, untellable
— now I bid farewell to you,
wishing you fare well, but when
— when can we meet again?
Your west-going form is retreating,
gradually fading out of my sight,
when misty hills rise upon foggy hills.

Translator: Zhang Zhizhong

你的微笑是我的微風

林明理

今年嚴冬我們遙望遠方

談詩，相顧而笑

你説

你的微笑是我的微風

那想來就是最真的自然了

我要説你是唯一的而我正費思

想你恰似一小片海域

卻和廣闊的海洋相隔

是的，我們在溫和的沙灘上走

空氣中有海藻的味道

Your Smile Is a Breeze for Me

Lin Mingli

In this winter we look afar into the distance

Talking about poetry, smiling at each other

You say

Your smile is a breeze for me

Upon thinking, it is the most sincere nature

I want to say you are the only one; I am thinking hard

You are like a small patch of sea

Which is separated by the vast ocean

Yes, we are walking on the tranquil beach

There is the smell of seaweed in the air.

Translator: Zhang Zhizhong

23. 微 涼

宋‧寇准

高桐深密間幽篁，
乳燕聲稀夏日長。
獨坐水亭風滿袖，
世間清景是微涼。

23. Slight Cool

Kou Zhun [Song Dynasty]

A dense bamboo grove,
penetrative and profound,
　　is intermingled with
　　　　towering phoenix trees;
　thickening and darkening
as summer advances
　　into its height, the grove
　　　is a muffler of the
　chirping of young
swallows. Sitting alone
　　in the wind-blown water-
　　　side pavilion, I feel my
　sleeves keep fluttering
in the breeze, when a
　　slight cool brings pure
　　　　scene to human world.

夏日慵懶的午後

林明理

有座被鳥雀和
蓮花簇擁的小森林，
湖面似透鏡，
雲終於落下來。
我踮起腳尖，
按下快門的一瞬，
細碎的陽光是背景，
天空無語，卻令我沉迷。
我以為自己可以及時
找到真理和歡樂，
那遺世的孤獨
已離開很遠；
風總是靜靜地吹，
在這夏日慵懶的午後。

A Languid Summer Afternoon

Lin Mingli

There is a little forest,
Surrounded by birds and lotus flowers;
The lake surface is like a mirror
Upon which clouds finally fall.
I stand on tiptoe,
And when I press the shutter of my camera,
The fragmented sunlight as the background,
I am enthralled by the wordless sky.
I believe I can find truth
And happiness in time,
When the loneliness of the world
Has been far away.
The wind is always blowing gently,
In the languid summer afternoon.

Translator: Zhang Zhizhong

24. 秋詞二首（一）

唐・劉禹錫

自古逢秋悲寂寥，
我言秋日勝春朝。
晴空一鶴排雲上，
便引詩情到碧霄。

24. Two Poems About Autumn (No. 1)

Liu Yuxi [Tang Dynasty]

Since ancient times,

autumn is redolent of

a touch of sorrow, but

I love autumn better

than spring days —

a crane is climbing

the boundless blue sky

through clouds after clouds,

when my poetic sentiment

is inspired heavenward.

Translator: Zhang Zhizhong

十月秋雨

林明理

我記得你凝視的眼神。
你一頭微捲的褐髮，思維沉靜。
微弱的風拖曳在樹梢張望，
落葉在我腳底輕微地喧嚷。

你牽著我的手在畫圓，卻選擇兩平線：
銀河的一邊、數彎的濃霧、飛疾的電光，
那是我無法掌握前進的歸向，
我驚散的靈魂潛入了無明。

在山頂望夜空。從鐵塔遠眺到田野。
你的距離是無間、是無盡、是回到原點！
曉色的樺樹在你眼底深處雄立。
秋天的雨點在你身後串成連珠……

Autumn Rain in October

Lin Mingli

I still remember your gaze,
your brown curls, your quiet thoughts,
gentle wind lingering in the treetops,
falling leaves whispering under my feet.

You take my hand to draw a circle, but you choose
two lines:
beyond the Milky Way, heavy fog, flying sheets of
lightning.
I cannot keep moving forward,
And my surprised soul dives into endless dark.

Looking into night sky from the hilltop, and from
the iron tower into the field.
Your distance is unmeasurable, endless, back to the
original point!
The morning birch is standing erect in your eyes.
The autumn raindrops cluster into strings of beads
behind you ….

Translator: Zhang Zhizhong

25. 鳥鳴澗

唐・王維

人閑桂花落，
夜靜春山空。
月出驚山鳥，
時鳴春澗中。

25. The Deep Peace of Spring Dale

Wang Wei [Tang Dynasty]

The falling of osmanthus flowers, witnessed by idlers,

is the only sound that breaks in upon the uniform

tranquility of the empty spring mountain

veiled in still night. The occasional

twittering of mountain birds,

startled by moonrise,

breaks the deep

peace of the

spring

dale.

Translator: Zhang Zhizhong

重歸自然

林明理

這一片淺水海域
孕育出的野外天堂，
蝴蝶、小動物和鳥
充滿著多彩季節的旋律。

夏夜
以溫柔之風環繞島嶼，
外界紛紜和帶痛的思緒
似乎都離得很遠。

只有圓月在林梢慢移，
而我的心
也在尋求重歸自然
──寧靜的聲音。

Return to Nature

Lin Mingli

This stretch of shallow water area

Gives birth to a paradise in wilderness;

Butterflies, small animals and birds

Are full of the melody of a colorful season.

Summer night

The gentle wind embraces the island;

Eternal strife and painful thoughts

Seem to befar away.

Only the moon is moving slowly at the tip of the

forest,

And my heart

Is also seeking to return to nature

— The sound of quietude.

Translator: Zhang Zhizhong

26. 烏衣巷

唐・劉禹錫

朱雀橋邊野草花，
烏衣巷口夕陽斜。
舊時王謝堂前燕，
飛入尋常百姓家。

26. Lane of Black Clothes

Liu Yuxi [Tang Dynasty]

Wild grass grows lush
by the Bridge of Birds;
   the setting sun slants
over the Lane of Black
Clothes. Swallows,
   wheeling and lingering
by painted eves of yore,
are now flying into
   common homes.

Translator: Zhang Zhizhong

夕陽落在沙丘之後

林明理

數百隻鵜鶘飛起

飛進那寒冷的海岸，

回到那入海的泥地

整個冬天都將繁殖著。

而艾爾湖湖面和鹽盤，

讓我的思緒隨之而去；

我願是

桉樹下乘涼的野馬那樣生活。

在我所選擇的方向奔跑，

微笑地站著，好像整片天空

──屬我一個。

註：艾爾湖，是澳洲最大鹹水湖。

Sunset Behind the Dunes

Lin Mingli

Hundreds of pelicans are flying up and down

Toward the cold coast,

Back to the swamp bordering the sea

To breed the whole winter.

The surface and salt plates of Lake Eyre,

Carry my thoughts away;

I would like

To live a life like the wild horses under the

Eucalyptus,

Running in the direction of my own will,

Standing with a smile, as if the whole sky

— belongs to me.

Note: Lake Eyre is the largest lagoon in Australia.

Translator: Zhang Zhizhong

27. 醜奴兒・書博山道中壁

宋・辛棄疾

少年不識愁滋味，
愛上層樓。
愛上層樓，
為賦新詞強說愁。

而今識盡愁滋味，
欲說還休。
欲說還休，
卻道天涼好個秋！

27. Written on the Wall on My Way to Boshan

一 to the Tune of "Song of Ugly Slave"

Xin Qiji [Song Dynasty]

As a lad sorrow never
visits my mind — it is a
stranger to me. I love
ascending the stairs,
more stairs, to a great
and greater height,
to feign sorrow to produce
lovey-dovey literary pieces.

Nowadays I am often
overcome by ennui and
grief, the sight of what
is beautiful in nature
from a great height fails
to interest my heart and
communicate elasticity
to my spirits — for a reason
that I cannot phrase,
but I only sigh with feeling:
oh, what — what an autumn
— it's crisp and cool!

Translator: Zhang Zhizhong

早 霧

林明理

窗臺外，遠處木犁
空蕩蕩地
單掛在田壟
那兒，山烟之上
你瞅著我，有好一陣
接著，我倚上沙發閉上眼睛
有如羊在霧中
想起了那年
瑟縮的二月
——透一股清冷

那是多久前的事兒了
我懷疑地問：
夜裏吹亂我頭髮的風
從上面經過　回聲
落滿了河谷
過去的日子彷彿
一切都很重要
又都不很重要
就像早霧頑皮地溜走
說了等於沒說

Morning Fog

Lin Mingli

Outside the window, the wooden plow beyond
Deserted
On the field ridge
There, above the smoke of the mountain
You look at me, for a great while
Then, leaning on the sofa, I close my eyes
Like a sheep in the fog
Reminding me of that year
The cold shivering February
— A spell of transparently cold

That was something long long ago
I ask doubtfully:
The night wind which blows my disheveled hair
From above　echoing
Filling the valley
The past days seem
Everything is important
And not so important
Just like the morning fog gliding away
Something said is something unsaid

Translator: Zhang Zhizhong

28. 答 人

唐・太上隱者

偶來松樹下，
高枕石頭眠。
山中無曆日，
寒盡不知年。

28. In Reply

A Recluse [Tang Dynasty]

Occasionally I come

under a pine tree, to sleep

while pillowing upon

a stone. In the mountain

there is no calendar:

coldness ending, without

knowledge of the year.

Translator: Zhang Zhizhong

我一直在看著你

林明理

我看見一顆星子在懸崖上
在這冬季黑夜
俯視我眼底的深情。

我看見一小苔蘚在瀑布旁
感覺到越是稀少的物種
在自然界裡越難以親近。

我看見冰層逐年融化，消失。
生命短暫。我
卻一直想這樣看著你，永遠幸福。

I Am Always Watching You

Lin Mingli

I see a star against the cliff
In the dark wintry night
Overlooking the deep affections in my eyes

I see a small moss near the waterfall
And I feel the rarer the species in nature
The more difficult of approach.

I see the ice layers thawing and disappearing year
after year.
Life is so short. I
Just want to watch you thus, forever and ever to be
happy.

Translator: Zhang Zhizhong

29. 天淨沙・秋思

元・馬致遠

枯藤老樹昏鴉，
小橋流水人家，
古道西風瘦馬。
夕陽西下，
斷腸人在天涯。

29. Autumnal Thoughts

— to the Tune of "Pure Sand under the Clear Sky"

Ma Zhiyuan [Yuan Dynasty]

Withered vines on an old tree, where dusk crows crow,

a small bridge under which water is babbling, around homey homes,

an ancient trail along which a gaunt horse is trotting in the west wind;

the sun is on the westering,

and the straggler: a gloomy silhouette against the skyline.

Translator: Zhang Zhizhong

金池塘

林明理

風在追問杳然的彩雲
遠近的飛燕在山林的
背影掠過

羞澀的石榴
醉人的囈語，出沒的白鵝
伴著垂柳戲波

秋塘月落
鏡面，掛住的
恰是妳帶雨的明眸

Golden Pond

Lin Mingli

The wind is chasing colorful clouds into the distance
Far and near the shadows of the swallows
Are flitting by

The shy pomegranates
Intoxicating flapdoodle, white geese appearing
Frolicking under weeping willows

The moon setting in the autumn pond
The mirror surface, hanging
Your fair face moist with rain

Translator: Zhang Zhizhong

30. 旅夜書懷

唐・杜甫

細草微風岸，
危檣獨夜舟。
星垂平野闊，
月湧大江流。
名豈文章著，
官應老病休。
飄飄何所似？
天地一沙鷗。

30. Night Sailing

Du Fu [Tang Dynasty]

Riverside tender grass is dancing
gently under a breeze; a lonely
tall mast is nosing through a vast
sheet of darkness. A maze of stars
drooping over boundlessly
desolate field, the moon is
surging and swinging as the
great river is swelling and
undulating. The fame of a person
is established only from his literary
pieces? An official, pestered by
sickness and old age, resigns from
his post. Flapping, fluttering, floating,
what I am? Between heaven and earth,
I am belittled to a mere wild gull,
wheeling in the boundless emptiness.

Translator: Zhang Zhizhong

北極燕鷗

林明理

一群群，一對對

在雲層之上

飛過高山和重洋

飛過海灣和激流

——數萬里遠，

為了生存

為了繁殖

努力向前

在南極的浮冰上越冬。

冬去春來

兩極之路，

成為他們共同的方向，

勇者亦如此。

> **註：** 北極燕鷗（The Arctic tern）是候鳥，牠們在北極繁殖，卻要飛到南極去越冬，每年在兩極之間往返一次，行程數萬公里，是世界上飛得最遠的鳥類。

The Arctic Terns

Lin Mingli

A pair after another pair　a flock after another flock

Above the clouds

Flying over high mountains and oceans

Flying over bays and rapids

一 Tens of thousands of miles away,

To survive

To breed

Efforts are made to move on

To pass the winter on the floating ice of the Antarctic.

Winter gone and spring around the corner

The road between the South Pole and the North pole,

Is their same direction,

So are the brave ones.

Note: The Arctic terns are a kind of migratory birds that breed in the Arctic and fly to Antarctica for wintering. They travel back and forth between the poles annually for tens of thousands of kilometers, and they are the birds with the greatest flight distance in the world.

31. 虞美人

宋・蔣捷

少年聽雨歌樓上，
紅燭昏羅帳。
壯年聽雨客舟中，
江闊雲低，
斷雁叫西風。

而今聽雨僧廬下，
鬢已星星也。
悲歡離合總無情，
一任階前，
點滴到天明。

31. Beauty Lady Yu

Jiang Jie [Song Dynasty]

As a lad, I lend an ear to the rain in the singing house,
where the gauze curtain is dimly lit by a red candle;
as an adult, I lend an ear to the rain in a wandering
boat,
which rows on a wide river kissed by low clouds,
wild geese crying against the wanton west wind.

Now, I lend an ear to the rain under the temple eaves,
my hair growing grayed and grizzled.
Partings and reunions — to suffer the vicissitudes of
life;
the stone steps stay so constant,
to bear the dripping-dropping till the morning.

Translator: Zhang Zhizhong

倒 影

林明理

霧靄淡煙著
河谷的邊緣，
你的影子沉落在夕陽
把相思飄浮在塔樓上。

回首，凝視那常春藤的院落。
每當小雨的時候
淚光與植物，混合成
深厚而縹緲的灰色……

Inverted Image

Lin Mingli

Thin mist and pale smoke

The edge of the river

Your shadow drops in the setting sun

Yearning floating above the tower

Turning back, to look at the courtyard overgrown with ivy

Whenever a light rain falls

Tears and plants, mingle into

Dense and ethereal grey ….

Translator: Zhang Zhizhong

32. 蔔算子・詠梅

宋・陸遊

驛外斷橋邊，
寂寞開無主。
已是黃昏獨自愁，
更著風和雨。

無意苦爭春，
一任群芳妒。
零落成泥碾作塵，
只有香如故。

32. Ode to Plum Blossoms

— to the Tune of "Diviner's Song"

Lu You [Song Dynasty]

By a broken bridge beyond the courier station,
plum   blossoms   bloom   in   total   isolation,
unappreciated.
Unbearable: dusk deepens the solitary sorrow;
winds & rains add to the miserable spectacle.

No ambition to strive with anyone in spring,
in spite of envy from myriads of flowers.
When withered, faded, fallen, and mashed to dust,
the fragrance lingers, refusing to die away.

Translator: Zhang Zhizhong

樹林入口

林明理

時間是水塘交替的光影

它的沉默浸滿了我的瞳仁

雨沖出凹陷的泥地

在承接暗藍的蒼穹

一隻小彎嘴畫眉

正叼走最後一顆晨星

呵四季從不懂謊言

就像我的心啊

披滿十一月秋天

除了想你已無處躲藏

當太陽掠過樺樹上端

索性把思念變成一條小溪

讓重疊的濃綠時時潺潺鳴響

The Forest Entrance

Lin Mingli

Time is the overlapping shadows of the pool
Its silence fills up my pupils
The rain gushes out of the muddy pit
In the sky imbibing dark blue
A little hook-beaked blackbird
Is pecking away the last morning star

The four seasons never know lies
Oh, like my heart
Which is filled with autumnal tints in November
Nowhere to hide except thoughts of you
When the sun slides past the top of the birch
My longing is turned into a brook
For the overlapping dark green to always babble and
gurgle

Translator: Zhang Zhizhong

33. 贈劉景文

宋・蘇軾

荷盡已無擎雨蓋，
菊殘猶有傲霜枝。
一年好景君須記，
正是橙黃橘綠時。

33. To My Friend Liu Jingwen

Su Shi [Song Dynasty]

Lotus flowers have withered, one and all; even the rain
-proof lotus leaves have dried up and shriveled.
Chrysanthemum flowers, fading and drooping,
still brave icy cold with their stubborn stems.
The most beautiful season of the year,
remember, is the period of the end
of autumn and the beginning
of winter: oranges golden
and tangerines
green.

Translator: Zhang Zhizhong

你一直在我身邊

林明理

風雨過後
星星一樣璀璨明淨
飛吧，思念
在那兒——
在冬天的一個晚上

彷彿從地平線的彼岸
傳來了熟悉的聲響
那橫渡的月光啊
將不是虛幻
是我靜默的遐想

你一直在那兒
在薄雪紛飛的

You Are Always By My Side

Lin Mingli

After the storm

The stars are pure and brilliant

Fly, my yearning

— There

On a wintry night

As if from the other shore of the horizon

A familiar voice is travelling here

Oh the traversing moonlight

Fantasy no more

It is my silent reverie

You are always there

By the stove where

爐火旁
帶著我從未看過的
如清水般的目光

啊，我的朋友
像傳說中的神話
像風帆高掛的大船
轉眼便到眼前……
史詩般的圖像

There is a flurry of flying snow

With eyes limpid like water

Which I have never seen

Oh, dear friend

Like the legendary myth

Like the ship proud with a tall mast

Into the sight all of a sudden ….

The epic-like image

Translator: Zhang Zhizhong

34. 憫 農（一）

唐・李紳

鋤禾日當午，

汗滴禾下土。

誰知盤中餐，

粒粒皆辛苦。

34. Poor Farmers (1)

Li Shen [Tang Dynasty]

weed under the scorching
sun, their sweat dripping
and dropping. The rice
in the bowls on the table,
who knows, is the product
of hard toiling and moiling.

Translator: Zhang Zhizhong

靜寂的黃昏

林明理

一隻秋鷺立著，它望著遠方。

萋萋的蘆葦上一葉扁舟。

對岸：羊咩聲，鼓噪四周的蛙鳴。

它輕輕地振翅飛走，

羽毛散落苗田，

彷彿幾絲村舍的炊煙。

The Still Dusk

Lin Mingli

An egret stands, watching far away.

Among luxuriant reeds there is a small leaf-like boat.

The other shore, the gentle baaing of sheep and the croaking of frogs far and near.

Fluttering its wings, the egret flies away,

Its feathers scattering in the field,

Like threads of smoke from the chimneys of cottage kitchens.

Translator: Zhang Zhizhong

35. 蝶戀花・春景

宋・蘇軾

花褪殘紅青杏小，
燕子飛時，
綠水人家繞。
枝上柳綿吹又少，
天涯何處無芳草。

牆裡秋千牆外道，
牆外行人，
牆裡佳人笑。
笑漸不聞聲漸悄，
多情卻被無情惱。

35. Spring View

— to the Tune of "Butterflies in Love with Flowers"

Su Shi [Song Dynasty]

Red flowers are fading, faded,
　　　green apricots flaring,
and swallows are flying,
　　　when blue water encircles
one after another home.
　　　Willow catkins are thinning
out on wind-blown branch;
　　　sweet-scented grass, rooting
anywhere, can be found
　　　beyond the horizon.

The swing within the wall
　　　and the path without —
without the wall a passerby
　　　is walking; within the wall
lovely girls are giggling.

想妳，在墾丁

林明理

每年落山風吹起

是墾丁旅遊的淡季

但我總會想起妳

如同孤鳥

整夜不眠地徘徊在

月光覆蓋的礁岩上

The girls' loveliest gurgles
are swelling before gradually
　　dying away; in the heart of
the traveler, a sense of loss
　　is surging and swelling.

I Miss You, in Kending

Lin Mingli

Each year when the northern-east wind blows
It is the slack season for traveling in Kending
But I never fail to remember you
Like a lonely bird
Which lingers on the reef bright with
moonlight through the sleepless night
When I pick up a shell and put it to my ears

當我拾起貝殼，貼進耳裡
我就感到驚奇，彷佛
那座軍艦石潛過大海
瞧，妳長髮如樹冠的葉片般
柔美而飄逸
瞬間，如夏雨

蘇鐵睡眠著、白野花兒睡眠著
甚至連星兒也那樣熟睡了
只有沉默的島嶼對我們說話
就讓時間蒼老吧
這世界已有太多東西逝去
我只想擁有自然、夜，和珍貴的友誼

I always feel the wonder, as if I always feel the wonder, as if

That rock of warship has moved across the sea Lo, your long hair is like the tree leaves

Which is fair, elegant and beautiful

In a blink, it is like a summer shower

Cycad trees are asleep, and wild white flowers are asleep

Even the stars are also sound asleep

Only the silent island talks to us —

Let time age and old

Too many things in the world have disappeared

I only want to possess the nature, night, and valuable friendship

Translator: Zhang Zhizhong

36. 江 雪

唐・柳宗元

千山鳥飛絕，
萬徑人蹤滅。
孤舟蓑笠翁，
獨釣寒江雪。

36. River Snow

Liu Zongyuan [Tang Dynasty]

Hundreds of hills see no
flight of birds; thousands
of paths witness no human
trace. A lonely boat carries
an old man wearing a straw
rain hat, who is solitarily
　　angling cold river snow.

Translator: Zhang Zhizhong

致青山

林明理

我昂首
如伸向天空的長頸鹿，
千朵萬朵雲兒掠過，
從綠油油的谷地到無邊的海角。
古老的土地上已沒有任何喧囂……
在這裡，
時間靜止不動，
月朦朧，鳥棲息。

To the Green Mountain

Lin Mingli

I raise my head

Like a giraffe which stretches its neck skyward,

Thousands upon thousands of clouds pass by,

From the green valley to the boundless cape.

There is not a single noise in this ancient land ...

Here,

Time stands still,

The moon is hazy, birds at rest.

Translator: Zhang Zhizhong

37. 詠 鵝

唐‧駱賓王

鵝，鵝，鵝，
曲項向天歌。
白毛浮綠水，
紅掌撥清波。

37. Geese

Luo Binwang [Tang Dynasty]

A goose, a goose, another
goose: in a single file they
　　are singing heavenward.
　White feathers swimming
in green water, red paws
　　poking waves clear and clean.

Translator: Zhang Zhizhong

山 魈

林明理

那彩面皮膚

像是京劇臉譜

當牠吸引母猴時

——紫色臀部便更鮮豔了

在稠密的熱帶長林山中

牠選擇了自由

過小群生活

白天忙著果腹

夜晚伴星星睡覺

瞧，這奇特的生物

站在山崖向南看

到底人類在想些什麼

註：山魈，mandrill，是世界上最大的猴，主要
生活在喀麥隆南部、加彭、赤道幾內亞和剛果的熱帶
雨林中。目前由於偷獵和棲息地的減少，山魈正面臨
著滅絕的危險。

The Male Mandrill

Lin Mingli

That painted skin

Is like the facial types of Peking opera

When it tries to attract a female monkey

— Its purple buttocks are more attractive

In the dense tropical forest

It chooses freedom

To live a life of the small group

In daytime it hunts for food

At night it sleeps with the stars

Look! The strange creature

Standing on the cliff and looking southward

Wondering what thoughts are in human mind

Note: male mandrills are the largest monkeys in the world, living mainly in the rain forests of Southern Cameroon, Gabon, Equatorial Guinea and Congo. Currently, their survival is threatened by poaching, hence the reduction of their forest habitats.

38. 長干曲

唐・崔顥

君家何處住，

妾住在橫塘。

停船暫借問，

或恐是同鄉。

我倆相識絕非偶然

林明理

如首次展翅而飛的海鷗，

只想與你平行遨遊；

我會努力

絕不輕易墜落……

天空何其寬廣，為自由

我無懼黑暗和險惡，

只想沿著這路到潺潺水流。

38. Ballad of Changgan

Cui Hao [Tang Dynasty]

"Where do you live, sir?
Hengtang is my hometown."
I stop my boat, to ask a lad,
who may be my countryman.

Our Meeting Is No Coincidence

Lin Mingli

Like the sea dove which flies for the first time,
Just wanting to soar together with you;
I will make efforts
To avoid dropping down easily....
How vast is the sky, and for freedom
I do not dread darkness and danger.
I just want to follow the path to the babbling water.

Translator: Zhang Zhizhong

39. 蟬

唐‧虞世南

垂緌飲清露，
流響出疏桐。
居高聲自遠，
非是藉秋風。

The Cicada

Yu Shinan [Tang Dynasty]

Its tentacles drooping
to drink dew; its chirping
running out of the phoenix
tree. From a great height,
its singing travels far, without
the aid of autumn wind.

Translator: Zhang Zhizhong

棕 熊

林明理

空曠溪谷的邊緣

一隻棕熊

閒晃著，吃草

春天，歌聲輕輕掠過　　　　　有繪圖？

雪、土壤與樹

萬物也融洽於一切靜寂

牠，慢移在岩間

回想起再也無法感受的童年

靜靜等待鮭魚返鄉時

孤獨的影像

彷彿大地的史詩

A Brown Bear

Lin Mingli

At the edge of an open valley

A brown bear

Is grazing leisurely

In spring, the singing is gently floating

By snow, soil and trees

Everything is harmonious in reigning silence

It moves slowly between the rocks

Reminiscent of the childhood which cannot be experienced

Quietly waiting for salmons to return

The lonely image

Is like the epic of the earth

Translator: Zhang Zhizhong

40. 照鏡見白髮

唐・張九齡

宿昔青雲志，
蹉跎白髮年。
誰知明鏡裡，
形影自相憐。

40. *Gray Hair in the Mirror*

Zhang Jiuling [Tang Dynasty]

Great aspirations of yore:
gray hair sees youth wasted.
In the bright mirror, oh,
pitiable form and shadow.

Translator: Zhang Zhizhong

當你變老

林明理

不管你信不信

我篤定

當你變老

我仍會看著月光

傳遞祝福及

索取一個吻

是的，我們的相知

是非比尋常的———

我常想起曾經讀過的詩

並珍藏在黝藍的星空

它讓我歡笑

也讓我憂愁

而你就是原因

When You Grow Old

Lin Mingli

Whether you believe it or not

I am sure

When you grow old

I will still stare through the moonlight

To pass on my blessings

To ask for a kiss

Yes, our acquaintance

Is quite unusual 一

I often think of the poems I have read

Which are hidden in the dark blue starry sky

It makes me laugh

It also makes me worry

And you are the cause

Translator: Zhang Zhizhong

41. 題竹林寺

唐・朱放

歲月人間促，
煙霞此地多。
殷勤竹林寺，
更得幾回過？

41. *Bamboo Grove Temple*

Zhu Fang [Tang Dynasty]

Life is but a span
where years rush;
this site is fair
with mist & clouds.
Bamboo Grove Temple
is enchanting: how
many times can
we be visitors?

Translator: Zhang Zhizhong

寄 語

林明理

你的詩如是輕盈，
我把它寄予飛燕，
不管穿越多少千里，
已開啓想念之門。

Message

Lin Mingli

Your poem is gentle and graceful;
I send it to the flying swallows.
No matter how many thousands of miles they fly,
The door of yearning is always open.

Translator: Zhang Zhizhong

42. 絕 句

唐・杜甫

遲日江山麗，
春風花草香。
泥融飛燕子，
沙暖睡鴛鴦。

42. *A Quatrain*

Du Fu [Tang Dynasty]

Lengthening days see fair

hills and rills; in vernal wind

    flowers & grasses are fragrant.

Over mud and soil swallows

wheel and fly, on warm sand

    mandarin ducks are sleeping.

Translator: Zhang Zhizhong

原野之聲

林明理

在空中
或諸神的腳步中
時而愉悅
時而靜靜晃動

我從不期待奇蹟
也不感嘆歲月如流
能誠實面對自己
真正去努力
是唯一的信靠
恰如這原野之聲
使我安詳無憂

Sound of the Wilderness

Lin Mingli

In the air
Or among the footsteps of gods
Sometimes happy
Sometimes quietly vibrating

I never expect a miracle
Nor lament the passage of time
To be honest with myself
And to work hard really
This is the only faith
Just like the sound of the wilderness
Which makes me calm and peaceful

Translator: Zhang Zhizhong

43. 登幽州台歌

唐・陳子昂

前不見古人，
後不見來者。
念天地之悠悠，
獨愴然而涕下。

43. *Ascending Youzhou Plateau*

Chen Zi'ang [Tang Dynasty]

Before me, I see no
ancients; after me,
    I see no comers.
I am caught between
heaven and earth,
    experiencing a strange
feeling of microscopic
smallness. Oh my,
    boundlessness of the
universe — solitarily,
I shed sorrowful,
    lingering tears.

Translator: Zhang Zhizhong

你，深深銘刻在我的記憶之中

林明理

有一天
你終將會離我而去
再沒有任何事值得我悲痛
世上已無所希求
你，深深銘刻在我的記憶之中

也許
我不能為自己也無法為你做點什麼
撒下這把灰白粉末
從此之後
你是否重新找到另一個天地

我從來不是個敏捷的詩人
也不敢成為你的唯一知交
只在暖雨中
在黑夜
捕撈你的影子，回到我的腦海
就像期待春花回到大地的懷抱

You, Deeply Etched in My Memory

eLin Mingli

Some day
You are eventually to leave me
And no more things bring me sorrow
Nothing to desire of the world
You, deeply etched in my memory

Perhaps
I cannot do anything for you and for myself
After casting away this gray powder
Then
Can you find another world

I have never been a nimble poet
Nor do I dare to be your only confidant
Only in the warm rain
At night
To catch your shadow, back in my mind
Just like the return of flowers to the embrace of the earth

Translator: Zhang Zhizhong

44. 獨坐敬亭山

唐・李白

眾鳥高飛盡，
孤雲獨去閑。
相看兩不厭，
只有敬亭山。

44. Sitting Alone in Jingting Mountain

Li Bai [Tang Dynasty]

A bevy of birds climb the sky of skies,

to be gone, one and all; the lonely

cloud is wafting at ease, alone.

I never weary of Jingting

Mountain, which is my

favorite kind of scenery,

and the mountain,

never weary

of me.

Translator: Zhang Zhizhong

即便在遠方

林明理

荒漠雖然孤絕，沙水相依。
歲月如夢的漂泊裡
黑暗中我將繼續探索跋涉；
即便在遠方，越深入心的深谷
越瞭解真實的自己。
且讓歌聲迴盪成亙古不變的記憶。

Even in the Distance

Lin Mingli

Though the desert is solitary, sand and water are interdependent.

Drifting about in the years as if in a dream,

I will continue to explore by trekking in the dark;

Even in the distance, the deeper I walk into the valley of the heart,

The better I understand my true self.

Let the songs reverberate into a constant memory.

Translator: Zhang Zhizhong

45. 題詩後

唐・賈島

兩句三年得，
一吟雙淚流。
知音如不賞，
歸臥故山秋。

我心嚮往大海

林明理

大海有許多故事
悲傷的……
雀躍的……

45. When a Poem Is Composed

Jia Dao [Tang Dynasty]

Two lines of a poem
are composed in three
　　years; upon reading,
I shed two strings of
tears. If I fail to be
　　appreciated by a soul
mate, I would seclude
myself in the autumn
　　of my native hill.

My Heart Yearns for the Sea

Lin Mingli

Many stories lie in the depths of the sea
Sorrowful…
Joyful…

神奇的……
甜美的…
都離不開一個主題
——愛
它無需言語
也沒有現實的距離
只要一想起
便如風輕拂著
世界也變得清晰明澈

愛情也是一樣
不會一直都平淡無波
不論是神迷的
或是狂放的
它讓人受苦煎熬
也讓人再度堅強驕傲
只要一想起
有時讓人心酸
有時會揚起微笑

Magical…

Sweet…

All with the same theme

— Love

It needs no words

There is no realistic distance

Once it is brought into the mind

It is like being blown in the gentle wind

And the world turns clear and limpid

Likewise is love

It does not remain calm and smooth

Whether it is entrancing

Or ecstatic

It makes people suffer bitterly

While making them strong and proud

Once it is brought into the mind

Occasionally it saddens people

Occasionally it coaxes smiles from people

Translator: Zhang Zhizhong

46. 宿建德江

唐・孟浩然

移舟泊煙渚，
日暮客愁新。
野曠天低樹，
江清月近人。

46. Lodging by Jiande River

Meng Haoran [Tang Dynasty]

I pole my boat by a misty
islet; at dusk the traveler
is touched by a touch of
sorrow. The boundless field
lowers trees in the horizon;
approachable is the moon
in a river of limpid water.

Translator: Zhang Zhizhong

雨 夜

林明理

夜路中，沒有
一點人聲也沒有燈影相隨。
在山樹底盡頭，眼所觸
都是清冷，撐起
一把藍綠的小傘，等妳。

雨露出它長腳般的足跡，
細點兒地踩遍了
壘石結成的小徑，
讓我在沙泥中
心似流水般地孤寂。

我用寒衫披上了我的焦慮，
幾片落葉的微音，卻聽到
那連接無盡的秋風細雨
竟在四野黯黑中出現和我一樣的心急……

Rainy Night

Lin Mingli

On the road of night, no
Sound, no shadow of lamp light.
Far away to the trees on the hill, what is in sight
Is coldness and inanimation, holding
A small blue umbrella, waiting for you.

The rain tiptoes its long footsteps,
Tiny drops trampling
All over the stony path,
For my heart to be solitary
Like running water in the mud.

I use my humble shirt to cover up my cares,
The shivering leaves fall, to hear
The endless autumn wind and drizzling rain,
Beyond the gloomy wild with the same worry of me ….

Translator: Zhang Zhizhong

47. 玉階怨

唐・李白

玉階生白露，
夜久侵羅襪。
卻下水晶簾，
玲瓏望秋月。

47. Grievances of Jewel Stairs

Li Bai [Tang Dynasty]

White dew grows heavy
on jewel stairs, which,
deep into the night,
soaks her silk stockings.
Crystal curtain is let down
to shut out the light,
before she casts a lingering
glance at the moon.

Translator: Zhang Zhizhong

你的微笑

林明理

你的微笑，似橄欖林中的風
正好流入莫奈和他的花園上
而我不知道秘密是什麼
但我知道鳶尾花的香味
在最初的冬雪過後，便
從賽納河畔流到
我的書房

Your Smile

Lin Mingli

Your smile, like wind from the olive woods

Is running into Monet and his garden

I don't know what is the secret

But I know the aroma of the irises

After the initial wintry snow, it wafts

From the banks of Seine River

Into my study

Translator: Zhang Zhizhong

48. 秋浦歌

唐・李白

爐火照天地，
紅星亂紫煙。
赧郎明月夜，
歌曲動寒川。

48. Song of Qiupu

Li Bai [Tang Dynasty]

Heaven and earth are aflame
with the furnace fire, from
    which a rocket-shower of red
sparks are flung, chaotic with
wreaths of purple smoke scattering
    through the air. The cold river
is shivering and echoing the
songs of red-cheeked young
    men in such a moon-lit night.

Translator: Zhang Zhizhong

在那星星上

林明理

我望著花間雨露
像布穀鳥，掠過
潺潺的小河，而搖曳
在稻浪的，春之舞

Upon the Stars

Lin Mingli

I am looking at the rain & dew among the flowers

Like cuckoos, passing by

The gurgling river, joggling along

The waves of the paddies, dancing of spring

Translator: Zhang Zhizhong

49. 渡漢江

唐・宋之問

嶺外音書斷，

經冬複歷春。

近鄉情更怯，

不敢問來人。

寒夜的奇想

林明理

當午夜狂雪遠逸，

覆蓋楓樹的光澤

與甜夢，風不再咆嘯，

只有回憶帶著我繼續飄翔，

49. Crossing River Han

Song Zhiwen [Tang Dynasty]

News cut off from beyond the mountain,
all the year round, from winter to spring
and onward. My growing timidity
gets the better of me, as I
approach my home: I
dare not inquire
about anything
from any–
body.

Cold Night Fantasy

Lin Mingli

When the midnight snow flies far away,
Covered is the sheen of the maple trees
And the sweet dream; the wind howls no more,
And only memories take me in the continuous flight,

引我期待些什麼。

當愛輕叩窗櫺的時候，
它就像上天的賜福，
崇高而美好，
像突如其來的吻，
驚喜卻豪不做作。

我根本不想理解，
它為什麼總是來去無蹤？
因為，當愛歸來的時候，
它就像涓涓不息的小河，
你可以選擇追隨，──

卻無法改變它原有的渠道，
而我很清楚，
愛，有時像鴿子，
那咕咕聲，來自喜悅，
來自遠方迢遙的窗口。

Leading me into some expectation.

When love taps on the window sills,

It is like a blessing from heaven,

Sublime and beautiful,

Like a sudden kiss,

Surprising and unpretentious.

I don't want to understand it,

Why does it always come and go without a trace?

For, when love returns,

It is like a babbling river.

You can choose to follow it —

But its original channel cannot be changed,

And I know it very well.

Love, sometimes like a dove,

The cooing, out of joy,

From a dim and distant window.

Translator: Zhang Zhizhong

50. 勞勞亭

唐·李白

天下傷心處，
勞勞送客亭。
春風知別苦，
不遣柳條青。

50. The Parting Pavilion

Li Bai [Tang Dynasty]

The most heartbreaking
spot is the Parting Pavilion.
Even the spring wind
knows the pain: the willow
twig is not greened lest it be
broken as a token of parting.

Translator: Zhang Zhizhong

懷 鄉

林明理

在我飄泊不定的生涯裡
曾掀起一個熟悉的聲音
但不久便重歸寂靜

它從何而來？
竟使我深深的足跡追影不及……
游啄的目光分離成渺遠的印記
每一步都是那麼堅定無疑

呵，我心戚戚
那是深夜傳來淒清的弦子
我識得，但如何把窺伺的黎明蒙蔽

Homesickness

Lin Mingli

In my wandering life
Once there is a familiar voice
Which is soon replaced by silence

Where does it come from?
And my footsteps fail to catch up with it …
Its wandering eyesight is separated into dim and
distant impression
Every step is firm and free of doubts

Oh, my sorrowful heart
Listen to the miserable chord from the depth of night
I know how to blind the peering dawn

Translator: Zhang Zhizhong

51. 秋風引

唐·劉禹錫

何處秋風至？
蕭蕭送雁群。
朝來入庭樹，
孤客最先聞。

愛的箴言

林明理

如果有人問
當愛情回到我身邊
噢，該如何想像──
又有誰說得清或膽敢說出
它真摯的美

51. Autumnal Wind

Liu Yuxi [Tang Dynasty]

Where arises the autumnal
wind? Rustling and moaning,
   it carries the wild geese.
The morning sees the wind
entering the courtyard woods:
   its first hearer is a lonely wanderer.

The Maxim of Love

Lin Mingli

If someone asks me
When love comes back to me
Oh, how to imagine it —
Who can tell it or have the courage to speak out
Its sincere beauty

它是一種魔藥
無法加以防備
如果愛情回到我身邊……
……它不是用來及時行樂
或瞻仰在虛空的晨星

而虛空的晨星——俱已消逝
卻總會又不經意地重現
它純粹是一種感覺
是世間無可比擬……
……亙古不墜的神話

當愛情回到我身邊
噢，我會記起你的微笑
它流過秋天的楓香小徑
從躲藏其間的風
到窺伺的星星

It is like a magic potion

Which cannot be guarded against

If love comes back to me ...

...It is not to make merry while one can

Or to admire the morning stars in the great void

The morning stars in the great void have disappeared,

one and all

But they will reappear inadvertently

It is purely a kind of feeling

It is unparalleled in the world ...

...The myth of immortality

When love comes back to me

Oh, I will remember your smile

Which flows through the Liquidambar Trail in autumn

From the hiding wind

To the peeping stars.

Translator: Zhang Zhizhong

52. 賦得自君之出矣

唐・張九齡

自君之出矣，
不復理殘機。
思君如滿月，
夜夜減清輝。

52. Since You Left Me, My Lord

Zhang Jiuling [Tang Dynasty]

Since you left me, my lord,
I no longer see to the fading loom.
A full moon, O, is my heart,
which wanes from night to night.

Translator: Zhang Zhizhong

思念在彼方

林明理

每走一步
像回到古老的時光。
即使陽光施予魔法，
讓雪的反射
從大海的地平線
到金色老城的冷色。
風　似乎在追尋什麼？
狂野地
吹遍岩床和河谷。
夜，是淒冷的……
相思如雪，濛濛落絮。

Yearning Afar

Lin Mingli

Each step forward

Is like going back to antiquity.

Even if the sun exerts magic,

For the reflection of the snow

From the horizon of the sea

To the cold color of the golden old town.

What is the wind pursuing?

It sweeps wildly

Across the rocky bed and river valley.

The night is cold ...

Yearning, like snow, falls ceaselessly.

Translator: Zhang Zhizhong

53. 拜新月

唐‧李端

開簾見新月，
即便下階拜。
細語人不聞，
北風吹羅帶。

53. Praying to a New Moon

Li Duan [Tang Dynasty]

The rolled-up screen
reveals a new moon,
    when she walks down
the stairs to pray. She
keeps moving her lips
    in silent prayer, while
the green sash round
her waist is fluttering
    in the north wind.

Translator: Zhang Zhizhong

我不嘆息、注視和嚮往

林明理

古老的村塘

凝碧在田田的綠荷上

我們曾經雀躍地踏遍它倒影的淺草

看幾隻白鴨

從水面銜起餘光

一個永遠年輕却不再激越的回音

在所有的漣漪過後　猶響

I Do Not Sigh, Gaze or Yearn

Lin Mingli

The ancient pond in the village

Green lotus leaves upon green lotus leaves

We have ever cheerfully trodden on its reflected weeds

To see a few white ducks

Picking up the setting sunlight from the water

An echo forever young yet without passion

Still resounding after all the ripples disappear

Translator: Zhang Zhizhong

54. 宿駱氏亭寄懷雍崔袞

唐・李商隱

竹塢無塵水檻清，
相思迢遞隔重城。
秋陰不散霜飛晚，
留得枯荷聽雨聲。

54. To Cui Gun While Lodging at Mr. Luo's Mansion

Li Shangyin [Tang Dynasty]

The dock shaded by bamboo is free
of dust; water-side towers are quiet.
My yearning soars afar, over towns
after towns. Heavy clouds linger
in autumn sky; the time of frost
flying comes late. Withered lotus
stems still stand, and pitter-patter
of raindrops is mellifluous.

Translator: Zhang Zhizhong

山楂樹

林明理

我在暮色中網住一隻鳥
它有秋月般的暈黃
虹彩般的髮
我願意朝夕地守望
每當它迅速地
驕矜地
把一個白霜的山丘
圈在它的腳踝上

春神在我臂下休息
仲夜從我身邊溜去
我沿著小路沒有回頭
直想輕步接近它的孤獨身軀
冬風不停地呼嘯而去
但我只能前行
直到它帶回長長的回音：
呵，忘却你，忘却我……

－是動中無聲的安寧

Hawthorn Tree

Lin Mingli

In the twilight I have netted a bird
Its fluffy yellow is like the autumn moon
Its feather is the color of rainbow
I would rather keep watching it day and night
Each time it suddenly
And proudly
Ties the hoarfrost- covered hill
To its paws

The goddess of spring rests under my arms
Midnight glides away by my side
I walk along the path without looking back
Only think of approaching its lonely stature
Winter whistling and howling and passing
Until it brings back the long echoing
Ah, forget you, and forget me ...

— It is the silent peace in motion

Translator: Zhang Zhizhong

55. 憶 梅

唐・李商隱

定定住天涯，
依依向物華。
寒梅最堪恨，
常作去年花。

55. Remembering Plum Blossoms

Li Shangyin [Tang Dynasty]

Planted in the remote horizon, and
yearning for fair spring view, cold
plum blossoms are hatable: they
always open flowers of the last year.

Translator: Zhang Zhizhong

綠淵潭

林明理

若沒了這群山脈，恐怕你將分不清
通向另一片蔚藍的希望之船，
那裏黎明正在沾滿白雪的雲階上等你。

總是，在分別的時刻才猛然想起
潭邊小屋恬靜地下著棋，當晚星
把你從落了葉的岳樺樹後帶往我身邊，
別憂懼，我已沿著那隱蔽的淒清昏光
滑入閃爍的冰叢外虛寂的海洋。

Green Deep Pond

Lin Mingli

Without the mountain ranges, it is hard for you to
distinguish
The ship of hope sailing to another blue sea,
Where the dawn is waiting for you on the cloudy
stairs covered with snow.

Always, a sudden thought upon parting
Quietly playing chess in the pond-side cottage, when
evening star
Brings you to me from behind the leafless birch,
No worry, along the dreary faint light from the shady
spot,
I have slipped into the empty ocean beyond the
glittering ice.

Translator: Zhang Zhizhong

56. 絕 句

唐・杜甫

江碧鳥逾白，
山青花欲燃。
今春看又過，
何日是歸年？

56. A Quatrain

Du Fu [Tang Dynasty]

The white birds are whiter
over a blue river; red flowers
　　burn in green mountains.
This spring is fleet,
to be gone: oh, when,
　　when can I return?

Translator: Zhang Zhizhong

遠方的思念

林明理

我想寄給你，寫在潔淨的
白雲輕靈的翅膀上
在這不是飄雪紛飛的冬天

我想寄給你
豪邁而無形式的歌
以及充滿友情的琴聲

雖然祝福在心中，天涯太遙遠
當你的眼睛逮住這朵雲
你將懂得我唱出的秘密

Yearning From Afar

Lin Mingli

I want to send it to you, written
On the light wings of the pure white clouds
On this wintry day without flying snow

I want to send it to you
A heroic and formless song
And the notes from piano charged with friendship

Although blessing is in the heart, the skyline is too remote
When your eyes catch this cloudy blossom
You will understand the secret I sing

Translator: Zhang Zhizhong

57. 問劉十九

唐・白居易

綠蟻新醅酒，
紅泥小火爐。
晚來天欲雪，
能飲一杯無？

57. Inviting a Friend for a Drink

Bai Juyi [Tang Dynasty]

A newly brewed wine of Green Ants over a small

stove of red clay, in which a bright fire is blazing.

As it gets progressively darker, there is a sign

of snow in the gathering of darkness: would

you care to come inside the house and

surround the stove to warm yourself?

I will pour you a nice warm cup of

wine which is heated, to keep

the cold out, since it has an

exceptionally fiery

nature.

Translator: Zhang Zhizhong

請允許我分享純粹的喜悅

林明理

請允許我分享純粹的喜悅，
當暮色沉降
世界苦難無法舒解，
請允許我從風雪森林中
步向妳，像所有星辰，
像老橡樹靜靜守護更迭歲月。
沒錯，我將用魔法
把時間和空間凝結！
從現在出發——
且超過未來！

Please Allow Me to Share My Pure Joy

Lin Mingli

Please allow me to share my pure joy.

When twilight sinks,

The suffering of the world cannot be relieved,

Please allow me from the snowy forest

To walk toward you, like all the stars,

Like the old oak tree quietly guarding the changing

years.

Yes, I will use magic

To freeze time and space!

Start from now on —

And beyond the future!

Translator: Zhang Zhizhong

58. 彈 琴

唐・劉長卿

泠泠七弦上，
靜聽松風寒。
古調雖自愛，
今人多不彈。

58. Lute Playing

Liu Changqing [Tang Dynasty]

From the seven strings

which are cool, clear,

and far-reaching,

cold wind is heard

to be blowing

through pines.

Though I love

this old ditty,

people nowadays

refuse to play it.

Translator: Zhang Zhizhong

淵 泉

林明理

涼晨中
我聽見流泉就在前方
彷若一切拂逆與困厄
全都無懼地漂走

一隻信鴿在白樺樹林頻頻
投遞
春的祭典

我相信悲傷的愛情
它隨著蒼海浮光
有時擱淺在礁岸
隨沙礫嘎啦作響

Deep Spring

Lin Mingli

In the cool morning
I hear the flowing spring ahead
As if all distresses and frustrations
Have floated away fearlessly

In the silver birch a carrier-pigeon
Frequently delivers
The sacrifice of spring

I believe in the melancholy love
It drifts along with the shimmering sea
Sometimes it runs aground by the rocky shore
Uttering a clacking sound from the gravel

Translator: Zhang Zhizhong

59. 早發白帝城

唐・李白

朝辭白帝彩雲間，
千里江陵一日還。
兩岸猿聲啼不住，
輕舟已過萬重山。

59. Morning Departure from White King City

Li Bai [Tang Dynasty]

The morning sees me taking leave of White King City,
which is crowned with clouds and, on the selfsame
day, I reach Jiangling, which is hundreds of
miles away. The crying of monkeys, all
the way along the banks, is barely
imperceptible by the ear, when
miles and miles speed past,
my boat passing through
thousands of
mountains.

Translator: Zhang Zhizhong

科隆大教堂

林明理

多美的哥德式教堂！

從東岸眺望——

上方，尖塔、星辰、灰藍

下方，河身、橋影、晃蕩

數百年過去了

它仍是西方重要的祭壇

沉睡在星空的樂曲上

*在德國萊茵河畔的科隆大教堂 Cologne Cathedral 是世界第三高的教堂，也是世界第三大哥德式教堂，被列名為「世界文化遺產」之一。

Cologne Cathedral

Lin Mingli

How spectacular is the Gothic church!

Looking from the east coast —

Above, steeple, stars, greyish blue

Below, the river, shadow of the bridge, waving and dancing

Hundreds of years have passed

It is still an important altar of the West

Slumbering in the music of the starry sky

* Cologne Cathedral is located in Cologne, Germany, by the side of the Rhine River, and it is the third tallest and biggest church in the world. It is listed as one of the "world cultural heritages".

Translator: Zhang Zhizhong

60. 望廬山瀑布

唐・李白

日照香爐生紫煙，
遙看瀑布掛前川。
飛流直下三千尺，
疑是銀河落九天。

60. Watching the Waterfall of Mount Lu

Li Bai [Tang Dynasty]

The Mountain of Incense Burner
is curling in thick purple cloud-
    wreaths under the sun, suffusing
        and lingering, now obscuring
and then rising above the dome
of the mountain, rendering
    this scene of beauty still more
        interesting. Viewed from afar,
through the coils of the foggy
mass, a waterfall, like a piece
    of white cloth, is pinned
        against the cliff; it flings itself
down from a great height
of three thousand feet,
    suggestive of the Milky Way
        tumbling down from heaven.

Translator: Zhang Zhizhong

季雨來了

林明理

所有島嶼不約而同地發聲
所有生物都在唱和——
在婆羅洲熱帶雨林中,
如你有雙好眼睛
又能聽見魚群的舞蹈
豬籠草的捕誘,樹鼩的竊笑
海龜也在漫遊著……
啊,我是我命運的主宰
我做我想要的
——自由和冒險;
而感受大自然的美妙也將
隨之而來。

註:婆羅洲(馬來語:Borneo),是世界第三大島,
亞洲第一大島。

The Rainy Season Is Coming

Lin Mingli

Spontaneously all islands make the voice

All creatures sing in chorus —

In the tropical rainforest of Borneo,

If you have a pair of clairvoyant eyes

And can hear the dancing fishes

The trapping Nepenthes, the snickering of tree shrews

The sea turtles are also roaming ...

Ah, I am the master of my destiny

I do what I want to do

— Freedom and adventurous;

And the feeling of natural beauty

Will follow suit.

Note: Borneo (Malay: Borneo) is the third largest island
in the world and the largest island in Asia.

Translator: Zhang Zhizhong

61. 楓橋夜泊

唐‧張繼

月落烏啼霜滿天，
江楓漁火對愁眠。
姑蘇城外寒山寺，
夜半鐘聲到客船。

61. Night Mooring at Maple Bridge

Zhang Ji [Tang Dynasty]

The moon setting, crows crying,

frost filling the sky; maple

    leaves along river banks,

lanterns on fishing boats,

sorrowful sleep. Outside

    Suzhou City, from Cold

Mountain Temple, the

sound of its bell travels to a

    traveler's boat in deep night.

Translator: Zhang Zhizhong

寫給科爾多瓦猶太教堂的歌

林明理

當我走向你，科爾多瓦，
走向古城，走向百花巷，
走向靜寂的猶太教堂，
走向聖潔的九燭台，
走向風中的荒涼聲響，
走向邁蒙尼德的雕像，
這時，你的沉默如葉飄落，
是我眸中晶瑩的水花。

啊，神啊，我的全能，
祢的慈悲光耀世道，
祢的福音在黑暗中浮現。
請支撐祢的子民，
撫平歷史的傷痕。

A Song for the Cordoba Synagogue

Lin Mingli

When I walk toward you, Cordoba,
Toward the city, toward the Flowery Lane,
Toward the silent synagogue,
Toward the holy nine candlesticks,
Toward the desolate sound in the wind,
Near the statue of Maimonides,
Your silence drops like falling leaves,
To become the crystal sprays in my eyes.

Ah, deity, my Almighty,
Your mercy shines on the mortal world,
Your gospel emerges from darkness.
Please support your people,
While healing the historical wounds.

在這和平的早晨，
聽我無聲的祈禱。
阿門。

　　註：科爾多瓦位於西班牙安達盧西亞自治區、瓜達爾
　　　　基維爾河畔，是哥多華省的首府，也是一個擁有
　　　　許多文化遺產和古跡的城市。其中的猶太教堂，
　　　　古老而莊嚴，牆上雕飾著希伯來文是出自猶太人
　　　　的巧匠邁蒙尼德。在猶太教堂內有座他的半身雕
　　　　塑，在附近的百花巷中也有一座他的全身雕塑，
　　　　他也是著名的猶太哲學家、法學家和醫生。

In this peaceful morning,

Listen to my silent prayer.

Amen.

> Note: Cordoba is in the Spanish autonomous region of Andalusia, the Guadalquivir River, and it is the capital of Cordoba province, with rich cultural heritage and a host of historical sites. The synagogue, ancient and stately, has its walls decorated with Hebrew by the hand of Maimonides, a Jewish craftsman. In the synagogue, there is a bust sculpture of him, and in the neighborhood Flowery Lane there is a full sculpture of his body. He is also a famous Jewish philosopher, jurist and physician.

Translator: Zhang Zhizhong

62. 回鄉偶書

唐‧賀知章

少小離家老大回，
鄉音無改鬢毛衰。
兒童相見不相識，
笑問客從何處來。

62. Returning Home

He Zhizhang [Tang Dynasty]

I left home as a boy
and returned as an old
　　man, whose native accent
persists, though my hair
is heavily tinged with
　　grey. The children, gazing
all over me in candid
wonder, ask me: "where
　　are you from, dear sir?"
Their eyes so merry that
they convey the impression
　　of mischievous boys & girls.

Translator: Zhang Zhizhong

曾 經

林明理

你輕俏得似掠過細石的
小溪，似水塘底白霧，揉縮
隨我步向籬柵探尋你的澄碧
我卻驟然顛覆了時空
熟悉你的每一次巧合

你微笑像幅半完成的畫
淨潔是你的幾筆刻劃，無羈無求
那青松的頌讚，風的吟遊：
誰能於萬籟之中盈盈閃動？每當
黃昏靠近窗口

今夜你佇立木橋
你的夢想，你的執著與徬徨
徬徨使人擔憂
惟有星星拖曳著背影，而小雨也
悄悄地貼近我的額頭

Once

Lin Mingli

You are brisk and gentle like the stream running
Over the stones, like fog over the pond, shrinking,
Follow me to the hedge to explore your green,
But suddenly I turn time and space up and down,
To be familiar with every coincidence of yours.

Your smile is like a half-done painting;
A few strokes make your purity, free and fetterless.
Eulogy of the pine trees, singing of the wind:
Who can twinkle in the noises? Whenever
Dusk approaches the window.

Tonight you stand on the wooden bridge;
Your dream, your persistence and hesitance,
Which makes me worry.
Only the stars are pulling your shadow, while the light rain
Is stealthily kissing my forehead.

Translator: Zhang Zhizhong

63. 絕 句

唐・杜甫

兩個黃鸝鳴翠柳，
一行白鷺上青天。
窗含西嶺千秋雪，
門泊東吳萬里船。

63. A Quatrain

Du Fu [Tang Dynasty]

The liquid voices of two orioles in emerald
willows fall pleasantly on the ears, when
the blue sky is alive with a flock of
white egrets in flight. The window
frames snow through thousands
of years atop the West Ridge,
and the door sees ships from
East China which have
covered thousands
of miles.

Translator: Zhang Zhizhong

觀白鷺

林明理

他垂下了翅羽
立於水面的岩石中
就這樣巍然不動──
彷若沉思的天使
任蜻蜓在頭上盤旋
一群野鴨款款游過
按下快門的那一瞬
我的心在雨後的校園微笑
泛著一種簡單的幸福

Watching Egrets

Lin Mingli

He has dropped his wings

Standing on the rock immersed water

Without any motion —

Like an angel in deep thought

While dragonflies are circling above his head

A group of mallards are swimming by

The moment I press the shutter

My heart smiles in the campus after the rain

Brimming with a simple happiness

Translator: Zhang Zhizhong

64. 早 春

唐・韓愈

天街小雨潤如酥，
草色遙看近卻無。
最是一年春好處，
絕勝煙柳滿皇都。

64. Early Spring

Han Yu [Tang Dynasty]

The heavenly street sparkles
in a soft creamy drizzle, when
    the field is peppered with bits
of green: showing from afar
but disappearing on the approach
    of a traveler. This is the fairest
        view in fair spring of the year,
            before the imperial capital is
            steaming,
                    misty
                            with
            willows
        here
    and
    there.

Translator: Zhang Zhizhong

岸畔之樹

林明理

在我憩息的地方
岸畔之樹
像潺潺小溪
流經大片花田般
圍繞著我奏樂
在寂靜的森林內輕響

呵，那水貂似的髮絲
——我難尋踪跡的女孩
依著風的手指
忽隱忽現
快速地
問訊而來

The Bank-side Tree

Lin Mingli

In the place where I rest

There is a bank-side tree

Like a babbling river

Flowing across a large stretch of flowery field

Playing music around me

Gently echoing in the silent woods

Oh, the hair which is shining like a mink

— The girl whose trace is hard for me to follow

Following the fingers of the wind

Now appearing and then disappearing

With great rapidity

Coming upon hearing the news

In a blink

只一瞬間

黑瞳晶若夜雪

妳是海

你是樹心

不，不是，你是輕風吹拂的白罌粟

我的一切，繆斯無法增添你一分光彩

Your black pupils shine like night snow

You are the sea

You are the heart of a tree

No, no, you are a white poppy fluttering in the breeze

My everything, Muse fails to add a bit to your brilliance

Translator: Zhang Zhizhong

65. 望天門山

唐‧李白

天門中斷楚江開，
碧水東流至此回。
兩岸青山相對出，
孤帆一片日邊來。

65. Viewing Tianmen Mountain

Li Bai [Tang Dynasty]

The Heavenly Gate Mountain
is cut into two halves by
Yangtze River; the green water,
charging eastward, here turns
northward. Two green hills
are facing each other,
when a solitary sail sails
slowly from the horizon.

Translator: Zhang Zhizhong

霧起的時候

林明理

我們不期而遇
原以爲世上的一切都不孤寂
沒有客套寒暄
彷彿重逢是天經地義
然而
那熟悉的身影如晴雨
空漠地飄過在死亡中的廣場

霧正在升起
喧囂的人群　傘花晃動
街的盡頭　雨霧迷濛
空氣裏有著露珠的味道
一隻貓　蜷縮在樹底
似乎等待著什麼
久雨初霽後
十月的黃昏　風淡描而過

When The Fog Is Rising

Lin Mingli

We meet by chance
We deceptively believe nothing in the world is solitary
Without the exchange of pleasantries or polite remarks
As if meeting again is right and proper
However
The familiar form is like the rain or sunshine
Hollowly floating across the square of death

When the fog is rising
Noisy crowd and tossing flowers of umbrellas
The end of the street is misty with rain and fog
The air is redolent of dewdrops
A cat is crouching under the tree
Seemingly to be waiting for something
A fine day after the persistent rainfall
Dusk in October, the breeze blows gently away

Translator: Zhang Zhizhong

66. 涼州詞二首（其二）

唐·王之渙

黃河遠上白雲間，
一片孤城萬仞山。
羌笛何須怨楊柳，
春風不度玉門關。

66. A Border Song

Wang Zhihuan [Tang Dynasty]

The Yellow River runs afar
into white clouds; a lonely town
sits alone amid a mass of
soaring peaks. Why should
the minority flute blame the
willows which refuse to green?
Spring wind has yet to visit
beyond the Jade Gate Pass.

Translator: Zhang Zhizhong

帕德嫩神廟

林明理

坐在巨石柱旁的大樹下
想像老城是怎樣變成今日的樣子
怎樣貫穿時間的秘辛
我向巨大蒼穹仰視
河水依舊不斷奔流
密談著愛琴海的神話故事

註：奉祀雅典娜女神的帕德嫩神廟是古希臘文明的
重要史蹟之一，這座擁有二千五百多年歷史的
城市廢墟，座落在雅典衛城之巔，俯瞰著希臘
首都雅典。

The Patrhenon

Lin Mingli

Sitting under the big tree by the huge stone column
I Imagine how the old city has become the appearance
of today
What is the secret of passing through time
I look up at the boundlessly great sky
The river continues to run forward
Whispering about the myth of the Aegean Sea

Note: The Parthenon, dedicated to the goddess of
Athena, is an important historical site of the
ancient Greek civilization. The ruined city,
with a history of over 2,500 years, is situated
on the top of Athens, overlooking Athens, the
capital of Greece.

Translator: Zhang Zhizhong

67. 春行即興

唐‧李華

宜陽城下草萋萋，
澗水東流複向西。
芳樹無人花自落，
春山一路鳥空啼。

67. Spring Notes

[Tang Dynasty]Li Hua

Grass grows green and lush
beneath the city walls;
creek water flows now east
and then west. Petals fall
unappreciated from fragrant
trees, and the mountain is
overflowing with birds'
twitters, all in vain.

Translator: Zhang Zhizhong

義大利聖母大殿

林明理

鐘聲響了

群鴿飛落簷上

天空一片澄澈

這是天使與聖者的殿堂

我才剛踏進一會兒

陽光便細碎地灑落

像是給我光亮

享受片刻寧靜的時光

* 聖母大殿（義大利語：Basilica di Santa Maria Maggiore）位於義大利羅馬，是世界上第一個以聖母命名的教堂。

The Temple of Virgin Mary in Italy

Lin Mingli

The bell rings
A bevy of doves alight on the eaves
The sky is limpidity itself
This is the temple of angels and saints
Upon my stepping into it
Sunshine trickles and sprinkles about
As if to give light for me
To enjoy the momentary tranquility

* The Temple of Virgin Mary (Italian: Basilica di Santa Maria Maggiore) is located in Rome, Italy, and it is the first church that is named after Virgin Mary.

Translator: Zhang Zhizhong

68. 滁州西澗

唐・韋應物

獨憐幽草澗邊生，
上有黃鸝深樹鳴。
春潮帶雨晚來急，
野渡無人舟自橫。

68. The West Creek at Chuzhou

Wei Yingwu [Tang Dynasty]

Lovely lush green grass grows
by a secluded creek, above
　　which orioles are twittering
　　　　in the thick foliage of trees.
Spring tide, under the cover
　　of a sky which is blustery,
　　blusterous, and blustering,
　　　　is running in strong sudden
rushes of water when the ferry,
deserted to be soulless, is
　　animated by a small boat —
　　　　nosing round by itself
against the current,
wildly and ineffectually,
　　amid a murky eddy
　　　　of torrential water.

Translator: Zhang Zhizhong

懷 舊

林明理

往事是光陰的綠苔，
散雲是浮世的飄蓬。
雞鳴，我漫不經心地步移，
春歸使我愁更深。

一花芽開在我沉思之上，
孕蕾的幼蟲在悄然吐絲；
它細訴留痕的愛情，
縷縷如長夜永無開落。

Nostalgia

Lin Mingli

The past events are the green moss of time;

Floating clouds are tumbleweed of the floating world.

A rooster crows, and I am amble carelessly,

When the return of spring deepens my anxiety.

A flower blooms upon my thoughts,

When a young worm is spinning silk stealthily.

It is telling its love story which is impressive,

Thread by thread like a long night without end.

Translator: Zhang Zhizhong

69. 送元二使安西

唐・王維

渭城朝雨浥輕塵，
客舍青青柳色新。
勸君更盡一杯酒，
西出陽關無故人。

69. A Farewell Song

Wang Wei [Tang Dynasty]

After the morning rain of Weicheng settles
the dust, rooftops of the inns are bathed
in softest blue, over which fresh
willows are waving lingeringly.
I urge you to drink, to drink
another cup of wine: beyond
the Sunny Pass, your westward journey will find
no bosom friend
like me.

Translator: Zhang Zhizhong

行經木棧道

林明理

黎明，帶著你折射出思想的芬芳來吧

跟著我，來吧，到石涼苔滑的棧道

在岩壁上像個僧侶披著雨帽

安謐中小青草比往年更茂更高

還帶著一切夢想沉睡的白蠟樹

冷杉和山毛櫸

用北方的民間歌謠

把夢想深藏在河流之心的夜空

來吧，把我也變一點兒

哪怕靈魂已凝成一座礁石

根根青草在波浪中起伏

Walking Along the Wooden Plank Road

Lin Mingli

Dawn, come with the fragrance reflecting your thoughts
Follow me, come to the plank road with cold rocks and
slippery moss
On the rocky cliff like a monk wearing a rain hat
The tender grass in peace is more lush and taller than
former years
Along with the ash tree slumbering with all dreams
Fir and beech
With northern folk songs
To hide the dream deeply in the night sky as the heart of
the river
Come on, give me a little change
Even if the soul has coagulated into a reef
A blade after another blade of grass is tossing in the waves

Translator: Zhang Zhizhong

70. 曉出淨慈寺送林子方

宋・楊萬里

畢竟西湖六月中，
風光不與四時同。
接天蓮葉無窮碧，
映日荷花別樣紅。

70. Fair Is the West Lake

Yang Wanli [Song Dynasty]

July sees the West Lake
presenting a scene that is
　　unique through the four
seasons. Lotus leaves upon
lotus leaves green the boundless
　　sky, and lotus flowers,
caught in the sun, are charmingly
red. Fair is the West Lake,
　　attractive in its way.

Translator: Zhang Zhizhong

西湖，你的名字在我聲音裡

林明理

西湖，你的名字在我聲音裡
來得多麼可喜
轉得多麼光潔
就像秋月與星辰
不為逝去的陽光哭泣
只跟雨說話，為大地而歌

我在風中，呼喚你
像新月一樣
升到山巔同白晝擦肩而過
四周是鳥語與花香的喜悅
而你宛若夢境
湖光把我的歌推向極遠處

West Lake, Your Name Is in My Voice

Lin Mingli

West Lake, your name is in my voice

What a pleasure it is

How liquid it is

Like autumn moon and the stars

No cry for the sun that is gone

Only talk to the rain, and sing to the earth

In the wind, I am calling you

Like a new moon

Which climbs to the mountaintop to be abreast with the day

All about is the overflowing joy of flowers and birdsongs

And you are like a dream

The light of the lake pushes my song far away

西湖，你的名字在我聲音裡

來得多麼輕快

轉得多麼遼闊

就像飛鳥與狂雪

不為逝去的陽光哭泣

只跟風說話，為山谷而歌

我在風中，凝望你

像雲彩一樣

升到深邃的繁星世界

輕輕搖曳，開始唱歌

而你在夢境邊緣

——我是追逐白堤岸柳的風

West Lake, your name is in my voice

How brisk it is

How vast it is

Like flying birds and crazy snow

No cry for the sun that is gone

Only talk to the wind, and sing to the valley

In the wind, I am looking at you

Like clouds

Which float to the profound starry world

Swaying softly, starting to sing

And you are on the edge of the dream

一 I am the wind chasing the willows along the embankment

Translator: Zhang Zhizhong

71. 漁歌子

唐・張志和

西塞山前白鷺飛，
桃花流水鱖魚肥。
青箬笠，綠蓑衣，
斜風細雨不須歸。

71. A Fishing Song

Zhang Zhihe [Tang Dynasty]

Before the Western Hill
white egrets are flying,
when perches are fat
in the water running
with peach blossoms.
Blue broad-brimmed hat,
green straw cloak —
no home return in the
drizzling rain slanted in
spells of gentle breeze.

Translator: Zhang Zhizhong

馬丘比丘之頌

林明理

我看見一隻老鷹徜徉於雲霧之中
這神廟即使是廢墟，也還是美的
加上那印弟安酋長的山巔之像
正聆聽遠方信號……它永不遺忘
來自星宿的各種訊息——從輝煌的
印加之城到現在的太陽塔日升之處

註：馬丘比丘 Machu Picchu 位於秘魯，是印加帝
國（Incan Empire）的遺蹟。這座古城坐落於
海拔 2,430 公尺的山脊上，地勢險要，有著「天
空之城」及「失落的印加城市」之稱。它是世
界新七大奇蹟之一，1983 年被列為世界遺產保
護區。

Ode to Machu Picchu

Lin Mingli

I see an old eagle wheeling in the clouds
The temple is in ruins, which is spectacular
And the statue of the Indian Chief atop the mountain
Is listening to the signal from afar … it never has a
lapse of memory
Various messages from the constellation — from the
splendid
Incan City to the present Sun Tower where the sun rises

*Machu Picchu, as the relic of the Incan Empire, is located
on the mountain crest with an elevation of 2,430 meters in
Peru. The terrain is strategically situated and difficult of
access, hence the name of "a city in the sky" and "the lost
Incan City". It is listed among the new seven wonders of
the world and, in 1983 it was designated a NESCO World
Heritage site.

Translator: Zhang Zhizhong

72. 感 懷

唐‧李煜

又見桐花發舊枝，
一樓煙雨暮淒淒。
憑欄惆悵誰人會？
不覺潸然淚眼低。

72. Reminiscences

Li Yu [Tang Dynasty]

The parasol tree is seen

to open old blossoms;

    dusk is murky with chilly

mist and dreary rain.

Leaning on the rail,

    heavy of heart, who

knows my heart? I

cannot help shedding tears

    while lowering my head.

Translator: Zhang Zhizhong

縱然剎那

林明理

湖面滿是薄染
將落的金光
讓淺玫瑰的雲霞
溶在銀波上
遠山幾行
有如紫精屏風的灰綠
遠比星空更柔然無聲的顫動
動盪的一桅風帆

半湖碧水
不若你明眸的閃爍
在影落波間
我感到宇宙只此一刻
春風拂來
我已幻成白楊之林
昂首矗立
在湖畔旁等候月光

Even in a Flash

Lin Mingli

The lake is veiled by a wisp of color
The golden setting sun
By the clouds of pink roses
Is thawed on silvery waves
Lines of the remote mountain
Like the greyish-green of an amethyst screen
More gentle and quiet shivering than the starry sky
The restless mast of a sailing boat

The blue water of half a lake
Incomparable to your shining eyes
In the falling shadows and waves
I feel the only flash in the universe
The advent of spring breeze
I have fantasized into a forest of poplars
Standing tall and proud
Awaiting moonlight by the lake

Translator: Zhang Zhizhong

73. 自君之出矣

唐・陳叔達

自君之出矣，
紅顏轉憔悴。
思君如明燭，
煎心且銜淚。

73. Since You Left Me

Chen Shuda [Tang Dynasty]

Since you left me,
my lord, my fair face
　　starts to fade and,
my heart is like
a candle, burning
　　and shedding tears.

Translator: Zhang Zhizhong

葛根塔拉草原之戀

林明理

雖然不是我的故土，
卻讓我遐思萬千，
草原未曾衰老，
胡楊憂傷如前。

每當盛夏之季，
野馬賓士勝似行雲，
營盤歌舞宛如嘉年華會，
駝鈴響過逐香之路，
神州飛船鑲入眼簾。

馬頭琴在帳外的蒼茫中浮動，
傳說中的傳說使我迷戀，

Love of Gegen Tara Prairie

Lin Mingli

Though not my homeland,

It evokes thousands of reveries.

The prairie has not grown old,

And the poplars are as sorrowful as before.

Whenever at the height of summer,

Wild horses run like swift clouds.

Singing and dancing at the camp is like a carnival;

The camel bells jingle along the fragrant road.

The Shenzhou spacecraft is embedded in the eyes.

The horse head string instrument is floating in the
dusk without the tent,

And the legendary folktales vastly intoxicate me.

這是天堂的邊界，還是繆斯的樂園？

還是我無言的讚歎枯守著期盼的誓約。

Is this the edge of heaven, or the garden of Muse?

Or my silent admiration is vainly waiting for the expected vow?

Translator: Zhang Zhizhong

74. 渡湘江

唐‧杜審言

遲日園林悲昔遊，
今春花鳥作邊愁。
獨憐京國人南竄，
不似湘江水北流。

74. *Crossing Xiangjiang River*

Du Shenyan [Tang Dynasty]

Lamentable is the scene
where I roam and play
in the garden; this spring
the birds' twitters elicit
my sorrow in the frontier.
Secretly I pity people
fleeing southward from
the capital, unlike the water
of Xiangjiang River, which
is flowing northward.

Translator: Zhang Zhizhong

四月的夜風

林明理

悠悠地，略過松梢

充滿甜眠和光，把地土慢慢蘇複

光浮漾起海的蒼冥

我踱著步。水聲如雷似的

切斷夜的偷襲

我聽見

野鳩輕輕地低喚，與

唧唧的蟲兒密約

古藤下，我開始想起

去年春天。你側著頭

回眸望一回，你是凝，是碧翠

是一莖清而不寒的睡蓮！

The Night Wind of April

Lin Mingli

Leisurely, it passes by the top of the pine tree

Filled with sweet sleep and light, gently waking the
land

The light is rippling with dark green of the sea

I am fording in water. The water sounds like thunder

Cutting off the sneak attack of the night

I hear wild turtle-doves

Cooing gently, while

Having a tryst with twittering insects

Under the old vine, I begin to recollect

The last spring. You keep your head aslant

To cast a backward glance. You are the gaze, the
green jade

A stem of water lily which is clean and not cold!

這時刻，林裡。林外
星子不再窺視於南窗
而我豁然瞭解：
曾經有絲絲的雨，水波拍岸
在採石山前的路上……

This moment, in the woods. And without

The stars no longer peer through the southern window

And I am suddenly enlightened:

Once there was a drizzling rain, waves lapping against the shore

On the way to the quarry mountain …

Translator: Zhang Zhizhong

75. 待山月

唐‧皎然

夜夜憶故人，
長教山月待。
今宵故人至，
山月知何在！

75. *Waiting for the Cliff Moon*

Jiao Ran [Tang Dynasty]

From night to night
I miss my old friend;
    the cliff moon is hanging
on high. Tonight my old
friend is here, but where
    is the cliff moon?

Translator: Zhang Zhizhong

記　夢

林明理

一整晚妳的聲音如細浪
泛白了黯淡的星河
我匆匆留下一個吻
在滴溜的霧徑上
或者，也想出其不備地說
愛，其實笨拙如牛

現在我試著親近妳　給妳
一季的麥花，著實想逗引妳
深深地在手心呼吸一下
如貓的小嘴唱和著相酬的
詩譜，叫我聞得到
那逃逸的形跡是多麼輕盈
──漫過山后

Memory of the Dream

Lin Mingli

Throughout the night your breath is like gentle waves

Whitening the dreary river of stars

Hurriedly I leave behind a kiss

Along the foggy path

Or, wanting to say unawares

Love is actually awkward like an ox

Now I try to approach you, to give you

Wheat flowers of a season, intending to tease you

To take a deep breath in the palm of my hand

Like a cat's small mouth singing reciprocal

Poems, for me to know

How light are the lost traces

— Overflowing across the mountain

Translator: Zhang Zhizhong

76. 浴浪鳥

唐‧盧照鄰

獨舞依磐石，
舞飛動輕浪。
奮迅碧沙前，
長懷白雲上。

76. The Wave-Bathing Bird

Lu Zhaolin [Tang Dynasty]

is dancing solitarily

over a rock, flying

over gentle waves.

Sometimes it is

wheeling over green

sand; sometimes it

is flying and soaring

beyond white clouds.

Translator: Zhang Zhizhong

如果我是隻天堂鳥

林明理

如果我是隻天堂鳥

我將永不忘記

回到故鄉

回到雨林這天堂領域。

所有生靈的樂趣

在沼澤和雲霧間

我飛上了

一樹高枝

獨自舞著，忘情的跳躍

還能遠遠地望得見

部落，從黃昏

到森林的盡頭。

註：2018 年 1 月 5 日觀賞 BBC Earth 影片介紹天堂
鳥（bird-of-paradise），有感而作。牠是巴布亞
紐幾內亞 Papua New Guinea 的國鳥。

If I Were a Bird of Paradise

Lin Mingli

If I were a bird of paradise

I will never forget

To return home

Return to the paradise of rainforest

The fun of all creatures

Between swamps and clouds

I fly atop

The branches of a tall tree

Dancing alone, jumping wantonly

I can see the tribe

In the distance, from dusk

To the end of the forest

Note: This poem is inspired after watching a BBC Earth
video introducing the Bird-of-paradise, a national
bird of Papua New Guinea on January 5, 2018.

Translator: Zhang Zhizhong

77. 春 日

唐・上官儀

花輕蝶亂仙人杏，
葉密鶯啼帝女桑。
飛雲閣上春應至，
明月樓中夜未央。

77. Spring Days

Shangguan Yi [Tang Dynasty]

Gentle flowers & riotous
butterflies & apricots of
    immortals; heavy clusters of
foliage & twittering orioles &
mulberry trees. Spring should
    have arrived at the Pavilion
of Flying Clouds, and in
the tower flooded with moon-
    light, the night is still young.

Translator: Zhang Zhizhong

想念的季節

林明理

飛吧，
三月的木棉，
哭紅了春天的眼睛。

飛吧，
風箏載著同一張笑臉，
心卻緊緊抓住了線。
飛吧，
楓葉輕落溪底，
行腳已沒有風塵。
飛吧，
我們都把心門打開，
讓光明的窗照射進來。

飛吧，
螢火蟲，
藏進滿天星，我是
沉默的夜。

The Season of Yearning

Lin Mingli

Fly,
The cotton tree of March,
The eyes of spring are red from crying.

Fly,
The kite carries the same smiling face,
Yet the heart holds tightly to the string.
Fly,
Maple leaves fall gently on the river bed,
When the walking feet are free of dust.
Fly,
We all open the doors of our hearts,
For the bright light to shine through window.

Fly,
Fireflies,
Hide yourself in the starry sky; I am
The silent night.

Translator: Zhang Zhizhong

78. 秋齋獨宿

唐・韋應物

山月皎如燭，
風霜時動竹。
夜半鳥驚棲，
窗間人獨宿。

78. Sleeping Alone in an Autumn Studio

Wei Yingwu [Tang Dynasty]

The cliff moon is bright
like a candle; wind & frost
wave bamboos from time
to time. The depth of night
sees birds startled from
their rest when, within
the window, a person
is sleeping by himself.

Translator: Zhang Zhizhong

憶友──Prof. Ernesto Kahan

林明理

你可曾諦聽故鄉花海的歌聲，那
榮美而威嚴的花兒
還有撒瑪利亞城，憂傷而平靜的眼眸
忽若愛神的懶散，
又似夜的寂寥。

你含笑在我面前，
滿懷安寧和自由。
那血脈相連的地土，回鄉的渴望
已深入你靈魂之中。
啊，七弦琴的律動──

註：1985 年初冬，prof. Ernesto Kahan 在其故鄉以色列
拍攝一張照片，並傳來電郵，有感而詩。

Remembering My friend—Ernesto Kahan

Lin Mingli

Have you ever listened to the singing of the native
flowery sea?

The beautiful and stately flowers

And Samaria, the sorrowful and calm eyes.

Suddenly like the languor of Venus,

Or the silence of night.

In front of me you are smiling,

Filled with peace and freedom.

The blood-linked land, the pining for home,

All have been deeply embedded in your soul.

Oh, rhythm of the lyre —

Note: In the early winter of 1985, professor Ernesto Kahan
takes a photo in his hometown of Israel, and sends it to me
through email, upon which this poem is inspired.

Translator: Zhang Zhizhong

79. 同裴迪和兄維別輞川別業

唐・王縉

山月曉仍在，
林風涼不絕。
殷勤如有情，
惆悵令人別。

79. *Leaving the Villa of Wangchuan*

Wang Jin [Tang Dynasty]

The cliff moon still hangs

at daybreak, and the cool

　　forest wind is on the blowing.

Lingering, and unwilling

to part; melancholy is

　　filling my inner heart.

Translator: Zhang Zhizhong

拂曉時刻

林明理

我們遇到迷霧
雖說還是冬季
湖塘微吐水氣
睫毛上也沾著露珠

細談中
一隻鷺在鏡頭前踟躕
這濕地森林
悄然褪色
萬物彷彿都在睡中

哪裡是野生天堂
如何飛離憂悒的白晝
我們啞然以對
只有小河隨心所願貌似輕鬆

At Daybreak

Lin Mingli

We encounter a dense fog
Although it is still winter
The pond gently spreads vapor
Dewdrops hang on our eyelashes

In the course of idle talk
An egret is hesitating before the camera lens
The wetland forest
Is fading quietly
Myriads of things seem to be asleep

Where is the paradise for wild creatures
How to fly away from the sorrowful daylight
We are wordless
Only the brook seems to be babbling at ease

Translator: Zhang Zhizhong

80. 詠螢

唐・虞世南

的曆流光小，
飄颻弱翅輕。
恐畏無人識，
獨自暗中明。

80. Ode to Glowworm

Yu Shinan [Tang Dynasty]

The glow of the glow-

worm is small, whose

wings are waving gently

and lightly. For fear that

it be ignored, it glows,

in darkness, alone.

Translator: Zhang Zhizhong

流　螢

林明理

穿出野上的蓬草

靈魂向縱谷的深處飛去

群峰之中

唯我是黑暗的光明

The Flitting Firefly

Lin Mingli

Through massy grass in the field
the soul of the flitting firefly flies to the deep valley
Among mountain peaks upon peaks,
Only the firefly is luminosity in darkness

Translator: Zhang Zhizhong